COMMON SENSE DESTROYS FAITH IN THE THEORY OF EVOLUTION

Written in Non-Technical Everyday Language

W. D. Cain

FIRST EDITION

ISBN: 978-1-953576-09-5

Library of Congress: 2021913814

Published by

Certa
PUBLISHING

3741 Linden Avenue SE | Grand Rapids, MI 49548

in Partnership with

Serve The King

P.O. Box 541149 | Orlando, FL 32854

www.ServeTheKing.org

Printed in the United States

Dedication

When one's decision to disbelieve is rooted in the deep resolve of the will, then it is unlikely that anything you learn will move your belief. But, if you can be open to the possibility that God lovingly created you, and the world around you, and put your brain in gear, then let's have an adventure and discover some really good news!

To victims of the pernicious God-denying and faith-destroying theory of evolution, and to their grieving families, we dedicate this work to all the lives that have been harmed or destroyed. "Lord may You see fit to grant that this brief insight shines into the great darkness that the *theory* of evolution brings. Destroy the empty confidence that it brings to so many, and the defenseless children presently under attack. May You raise up many valiant warriors to destroy confidence in the *theory* of evolution."

God has blessed me with a wonderful family, memorable parents, aunts, uncles, cousins, a beautiful daughter and two lovely granddaughters, and a son-in-law that is a great gift from God to me. As a husband, father and son-in-law he is an exemplar.

To God be the glory.

Acknowlegments

I am grateful and appreciative for the insights and discussions
with my dear friends at ServeTheKing.org.

Team members:
Demarick Patton, Don O'Rourke, Pat McGuffin, Mary Johnston,
Jeannie Johnson, Ron Heffield, Domenic Fusco, and W.D. Cain.

Everything we know, we have learned from others.
(Well… and from experience.)
Only God knows those He has used to pass along
the insights found here.
I am profoundly grateful to them all.
I wish I could pay tribute to each source
personally and individually.
May God bless them all.

Table of Contents

PART TWO: THE GOD FACTOR

The Status Quo

The *theory* of evolution has become dominant throughout the world. And you must go along or face the consequences. A part of our conditioning from science teachers and others may include suggestions that: God and religion are pretty much the same. That's a deception. When they discredit religion, they smear God along with it. They want you to believe religion and superstition are pretty much the same. Not even close.

They try and persuade millions that religion tends to have originated in primitive times…and children are pushed to see that "faith in God is not modern, and is out of date."

Most of the world no longer believes such a thing as witchcraft exists. They need to be told that in January 2021, a search for witchcraft on Amazon found seven very long pages on Wicca books and paraphernalia, every one of them serious and not poking fun.

Modern society is not aware that the spiritual dimension is real. Both "Light" and "Dark" exist in the spirit realm, and the

Dark masquerades as Light. You will be viewed negatively and cast out from the serious consideration if you resist the indoctrination. If you resist, you face not just their contempt and scorn, but the threat with being an outcast. The very nerve…thinking you know better than the scientists!

Within these few pages you can see how the basis, the very foundation for evolution is not science, but little more than conjecture, speculation, and wishful thinking. When the truth doesn't support someone's position, they are tempted to fudge. With no God in the picture, there is no reason to resist the temptation of creating alternate explanations of creation as the new norm.

It turns out that evolutionists, think the Garden of Eden is the fairytale; they are wrong! Au contraire. It is evolution that is the fairy tale. Eden is true history. And you can know it for sure.

The *theory* of evolution seems plausible only if your desire to flee God is so desperate that any other answer, no matter how irrational, is preferable.

There are two competing systems—one, easily supported by science, which has laws and requires a lawgiver. God the lawgiver. The other, is faux-science and speculation, the *theory* of evolution. They are two precise opposites and the authentic is the opposite of what is commonly expected. Surprised?

The public thinks science supports evolution, and therefore excludes God. Evolution is only "under the guise" of science, plus deception, and pushes to prevail in its war against God.

Let's equip you and your children with easy and self-evident truths refuting evolution.

Let's compare.

First system: God

God as creator is based on science, rationality, and common sense. Everything that begins to exist must have a cause. This is both scientific and common sense, and points to a Creator God. The "who created God" objection is answered by this insight. *There must, by necessity, be an uncaused first cause.*

Second system: Evolution

The attempt to adequately explain everything without God is based on conjecture, speculation and wishful thinking. And, upon reflection, qualifies as superstition. See for yourself. With no God in the picture, you are immediately forced to the irrational, illogical and nonsensical position of: "Nothing created everything!"

Isn't this what it comes down to? If evolutionists succeed in doing away with God, they must explain the "how" of everything, not merely beginning with the cosmos and the earth in place, complete with everything from which life "could" evolve. But where did it all come from?

Could the start of every bit of order we observe have begun with a big explosion in space? Give me a break! This is not science. It is *magical* thinking. It defies both common sense and experience, and yet is the basis and very foundation of evolution. It's the dominant view taught in schools and produces poisonous fruit.

Are you comfortable that much of the world thinks of a Christian as an ignoramus…that superstition, legends, and fairy tales rule you, and that you are stuck in the dark ages?

Should it bother you that the devil persuades the unbelieving world that Christians think they are better than them, and look

11

down on them, and probably hate them?

The concept of mirroring or reciprocity causes evolutionists to reflect back these negative attitudes. We must realize this and resolve that we will not give them any negative witness.

The world has been conditioned into thinking that science has replaced God in terms of what is real, of what can be known, and of what is authoritative. Children have been given the false choice of science or God.

We have the potential of armor-plating ourselves and our children with the truth. While the world receives evolution as liberating good news, it's actually false hope, leading to a bad ending! You can provide true hope and genuine good news, through insights you'll discover in these pages!

The world thinks science has proven that the Bible is not true, that the Gospels are mere man-made legends, that Jesus did not rise from the dead, and those who buy into such things are just simple-minded, and should go away and be quiet and leave the rest of us alone! All of these positions are refuted in chapters to come.

The science domain is, by definition, limited to the natural and the physical. It makes sense when you think about it. They claim that only the physical world is real….a conclusion they nowhere try to scientifically prove or justify. They can't "know" that nothing exists beyond the physical, but they can pontificate on it as if they do!

They will continue to get away with demanding everyone accept their views, unless you act. The question is a real one. If there were anything beyond the seeing, hearing, touching, tasting and smelling – how could you know it is there?

The facts are that only the physical can be weighed, measured, calibrated, confirmed and known. If there were a reality beyond the five senses – how could it be known? Are they right to deny the existence or the reality of anything beyond the five senses? That is a real question and it merits our best efforts in critical thinking. What is real? Let's give it a try.

The space you are in right now is likely filled with radio waves, TV waves, cell phone waves, magnetic lines of force pointing north, and gravity that causes the tides to come in and go out with predictable regularity, and who knows what else! These forces, though real, are not discernible through our five senses.

Wait a minute, they say. Those are all detectable with our instruments and we acknowledge their existence in reality. But because science is limited to what we can detect, our reality is limited to the natural and material world. There is no room for the supernatural here—our point exactly. They are operating beyond their jurisdiction when they talk about God!

Their subtle shift is *from admitting* that they are limited to the natural and physical, *to the assumption* and sometimes the declaration that only the physical exists. Can you and I know and prove the reality of anything beyond the physical?

Yes you can. You are *thinking* right now. Therefore, your thoughts exist. Are they real? Of course, they are. You are *valuing or loving* someone right now. Is that love real? Most assuredly. There is a wide range of concepts that exist, from justice to mercy to kindness and a whole host of other things. Are they real? It is self-evident that they are. Axiomatic. Is God real? Can we make the case?

Can we say that when science speaks about the natural and

physical, it is operating within it's jurisdiction, within it's domain? When it proclaims about the spiritual dimension and about the things of God – it doesn't know what it is talking about. Not to mention that it has no qualifications to speak of things beyond the material world.

Now who is the ignoramus?

What is behind the raw, thug tactics of coercion and intimidation by the group that rules the world? Evolution does rule, you know. They rule in government, in law, in the media, in sports and in entertainment, and surely in education.

The removing of God from our consciousness plays its part in broken homes and the failure that is the normal out-workings of Biblical principles as well as cultural and governmental decisions such as creating dependency on government, and incarceration, rather than Biblical discipline.

The *theory* is taught not as a *theory*, but as "settled science." Yet, this *settled science*, betrays itself by the routine use of mafia tactics to maintain its dominance.

There is a reason. Evolution has no proof of what it insists is true. Evolution rules not by science, but by the wielding of power, thug tactics, censorship, and repression of other explanations....in other words, by intimidation.

Let's look at how children can be equipped to answer some of the things listed above. We can tell children that faith and superstition are not the same, as they have been taught, not even similar. Superstition tends to be emotion based. Fears of thunder, lightning and storms are primitive attempts to understand things beyond the then-current, ability to explain.

The enemy of life wants to put all faith-based systems

into that category and dismiss them all. Evidence-based faith is grounded in reality and rationally defendable. For example, we rationally exercise faith when we drive in traffic, and when we eat or drink, that swallowing will naturally follow. Experience has shown that we can reasonably expect other drivers to observe the protocols of traffic. Experience has shown that when eating and drinking, that health protocols have been followed and we can eat safely from approved food sources. Is it a 100%? No, there will be some exceptions. But in general, it is rational to believe.

Is faith in God evidence based? Let's see for ourselves.

What is the truth-test for any truth claim?

"There is a Rolls Royce in the parking lot." This is a truth claim. How do we test it? By either verifying or falsifying it. We send someone to the parking lot. "The Rolls is there." The claim and the reality "correspond". The claim is true.

How does this work in proving God exists? There are basically two competing answers for all of existence; either all is from God, or all is from something else. We are not trained scientists, but we are not stupid. We, without help, can discern a great deal by the powers of observation.

We go out into the world and what do we see? We find a very great deal of *order* and *organization*. Does that order correspond to a big explosion in space, or to an intentional and purposeful "Mind"?

Looking further, we see that in addition to the order and organization, we find *fruitfulness* and *productivity*. Does that correspond to a Mind, or something else? The faith-destroying and God-denying *theory* of evolution has gotten away with deception, misrepresentation, labeling and lies for far too long.

Now we can do something about it.

The whirlwind we are reaping can be answered and refuted, simply and non-technically. Come and see. When my granddaughter was small, she told me how to eat an elephant. The answer: one bite at a time! We defeat evolution the same way... in small bites.

Our mission is to destroy confidence in the *theory* of evolution. How? Make children and adults aware of the deception one small, non-technical bite at a time. You can help.

Review and Reflect

Train yourself to question assertions; Evolutionists', ours, and everyone's. Evolutionists rely on the fact that most people believe their assertions without questioning them, even though they don't have the evidence to support their claims. We believe there are assertions that are self-evident, are grounded in life observations, in experience, and in common sense. "Nothing created everything?" I don't think so!

1

The Missing Standard Demolished Evolution

If you can know and prove that the evolutionists have no standard to justify assigning to, not God but to something else, then the pretense is obvious to all…and the edifice crumbles. If that happens, the believers are liberated from the gloom of the globally dominant false science that denies God.

We have all been conditioned, as far as evolution is concerned, to park our brains at the door and let someone else, someone we do not know, and have no reason to trust, do our thinking for us. However, the standard, the set of protocols, the criteria, the principles, the logic of "why" must, indeed be there. Anything else would be faith and not science!

If you assume that a standard exists, then you now must explain to yourself how come you don't know about it. Further you must explain how it is that no one else knows it. If a standard did exist, wouldn't you reasonably expect it to be prominent at every level, from the lower grades through graduate school? And would appear on every exam and in every textbook. And yet it is not there. Why? There might possibly be an answer other than the obvious. However, the obvious, common sense, self-evident, practical answer is...*They Don't Have One!*

You recognize that a Goliath rules the world. It defies all logic that evolution is merely a sham. (That would require all the genius of "the father of lies"!)

Now we understand the necessity of having to resort to censorship and quarantine of alternate views. This explains the curt and rude dismissal of Creation Science, Intelligent Design, and the like, rather than a demonstration of the superiority of their own view. That would require a "standard for comparison." Evolutionists don't allow a side-by-side comparison because they don't have the standard to justify assigning against God and for evolution. They can't say "see, here's why it makes sense."

No justifying standard reveals that the foundation of evolution is not "settled science" as everyone supposes, but lies and deception. It is only, and no more than a facade.

The ancient but still remembered principle of Nobelesse Oblige, implied the obligation of the ruling class to respect its subjects. The standing of the aristocrats was not challenged by the populace and, secure in their position, the rulers could afford to be polite. In the same way, truth has nothing to fear from challenges to the truth. If the evolutionists had a standard, protocols or criteria to defend their assigning against God, they could put other claims alongside evolution and show the world the superiority of their claims.

Having no standard, they have no other recourse than

to disparage, label negatively and derisively, and threaten to excommunicate from the rest of enlightened, civilized society. Such response is accurately characterized as "defensive". Not having anything rational to defend their views with, explains their pugnacious relentless attacks on any and all challenges.

It's not complicated, Evolutionists either have the goods or not. Every indication of the high-handed and authoritarian manner they have used so far would naturally follow in the brandishing of the conclusive, justifying standard of their system *if they had one*.

They haven't done it because they don't have it. This explains their use of an iron curtain of censorship and quarantine against anything that challenges evolution.

AND THE WALLS COME TUMBLING DOWN! It's the catastrophic collapse of the foundation of evolution.

They have no justifying standard, and, therefore no science, only bias and censorship. And most obviously, intimidation. The "science" that was thought to be the sure foundation of evolution is entirely missing. The absence of a foundation predicts a sure and certain collapse.

What if, from the very inception, before the first investigation began, the intent and purpose was to find ways to rule against God?

We have supposed that the people who began the quest were neutral, objective, trustworthy and honest. We assumed that they were operating within the disciplines of applied science and that they were not trying to prove a predetermined agenda to do away with God. All this hoped-for neutrality collapses unless there are justifying standards to support the conclusion that evolution and natural selection, and not God, are the proven explanation. Our giving the benefit of the doubt has been the basis of their fraudulent success.

If evolutionists have no justifying standard then they have no science against God.

Have they known this all along? Probably not the classroom teachers or the rest of the rank-and-file evolutionists, but the top five or ten percent very well may have. The resolve they have to believe in evolution in the absence of any justifying standards is not science but FAITH. And not just faith, but blind faith! Not evidence-based faith, but the absence of evidence. The audacity! The battle against God and His people based on sheer rebellion alone! Call it science and the world will believe.

A FORTRESS WITHOUT A FOUNDATION is a HOUSE OF CARDS!

Let's take a trip in our minds. It is in the lifetime of Darwin. His publication of *The Origins of Species* has rocked the world. We picture verification as scientists everywhere returning to their labs and have begun the rigorous process of re-evaluations of the data across the disciplines from Biology to Zoology. Tens of thousands of decisions will be made. Every decision will be decided against God and for crowning evolution as the new orthodoxy. (What are the odds?)

Let's look over the shoulder of the scientists, so to speak, and see what we can learn. The scientist is looking at an event, or process or outcome, or something else. He must make the decision. Is this the result of a God or something else? He checks and rechecks the data. Finally, the decision is made. He assigns it to Evolution. This is repeated across the spectrum of his area of expertise. And finds against God! (Again, what are the odds?)

The same is true across the rest of the disciplines from Agronomy to Zoology. The verdict is unanimous against God! Again, the odds are astronomically against this total outcome? Everything can be understood and explained by the Theory of Evolution? Wait a minute, you say. When we were looking over his shoulder, when the very first decision was made, we had a question that we did not get to ask.

So, we ask it now. "Why did you assign it to Evolution and not to God?" The scientist pauses, reflects, and finally says, "It just seems like the better explanation."

"Not what we are asking," we exclaim, "but what is the standard, or criteria or protocol you are applying to justify the decision to assign to one and not to the other? Surely, you must have a standard. There has to be a justifying standard. If there is no standard then, it is only a matter of personal preference.

Evolutionists deny the true discipline science demands. Their conclusions are sophomoric prejudice. And if not science and proof, then we must view evolution as a guess, devoid of factual authentication—a fortress without a foundation!

Is there a standard? What would it look like? Can you even conceive of what a standard justifying the assigning to one and not the other would look like? Have you ever heard at any time reference to such a standard? Wouldn't it be well known and likely even named after its discoverer? (Dr. Doolittle's Law of Discovery?) Doesn't it seem like if the evolutionists had one, we would all know about it? Wouldn't it be in every test, and every textbook, on every exam, taught at every level? Wouldn't we all know it, and be constantly reminded of it, and all able to quote it by heart?

Wouldn't the standard be made prominent and used authoritatively when the challenges of *Creation Science* and *Intelligent Design* and *Specified Complexity* and *Irreducible Complexity* are arrogantly and dismissively rejected? It's beginning to look like all they have is bluff and bluster, and it has been enough to win, in the eyes of the world!

The world and the church have meekly bowed to their pronouncements. Never suspecting for a minute, they don't have the science to back it up. We believe such was the case. But, without a standard to justify their rejection then you have, not science, but prejudice, bias, quarantine of opposing views and censorship! Wouldn't the results showing the superiority and vindication of evolution over the challengers be readily available everywhere on the Internet for all to see?

And since they haven't revealed the standard, isn't the most likely explanation that they don't have one? They haven't needed one. They have gotten away with it, until now. Will it continue? That is up to you!

The "promised freedom from God" is the reason they have gotten away with it. If the world could know, like you know, how much Jesus loves them, then that would make the difference. No longer would God be viewed as the caricature the devil has convinced them of!

You can make the charge that evolution is NOT science. It is fraud and presents itself only UNDER THE GUISE OF SCIENCE! And when evolution's foundation is known to be fraudulent, it collapses! There is nothing technical here. Everything is self-evident, commonsensical and lines up with your own personal experience. Therefore, you personally can argue this with anyone. It is not technical or complex.

And if you can explain it to a third grader, can a third-grade awakening be far be far behind?

2

Intimidation and Censorship

By government edict, children are required to attend school. For the tens of millions of children in government schools, forced indoctrination and brainwashing are the norms. You know the tactics—censorship of opposing views, and endless *under-the-radar* propaganda. For nearly a century, only one view of origins has been allowed in schools. Hint: it's not God. And it is they, not we, who are the censors! Their argument for evolution (never stated explicitly) is *everything came from nothing*. Really?

Indoctrination tactics that are well known are routinely used on children who are unprepared to resist them. INTIMIDATION: You will go along with the *theory* of evolution or face stigma, exclusion from the rest of us, banishment, and become a part of the outcast group of Neanderthals that think they know more than the scientists. Who dares to resist? No wonder so many young people have disappeared from the churches. The very atmosphere in secular schools and throughout academia, the ethos, is poisonous against the divine and the supernatural.

Of course, Evolutionists have no proof that only the material world exists. But, they get away with telling the children that is the fact! Our children daily face arguments like: "You know that all religions have their origins in antiquity." The evolutionists attempt the subtle undermining of things historical that are not really relevant to the question of the origin of the universe.

"You know, don't you, that science has proven its ability to speak authoritatively on all things," including outright lies and they get away with it! The children are given the false choice of God or science. Students are inundated with all the pseudo arguments against God, and for *so-called* science.

The arguments evolutionists use against God, such as "the suffering of the innocent, natural disasters and the hypocrites in the churches," are all straw men, and are pretexts in their battle against God. You can equip the children with adequate, simple nontechnical answers, timeless truths against dismissing God. Teachers, instructors, and professors are authority figures, many of whom relentlessly make their case against God, and for the authority of so called *settled science.*

The issue of hypocrites in the churches, does not so much raise the concern about whether God exists. Rather, people who raise those objections are really raging and protesting against the character of God. "I'm not going to serve any God who puts up with this!" This argument is the elevation of the person and their moral character over and above God.

Just as children may not understand the reasons behind parental discipline and decisions, our disbelief assumes there is no possibility that a benevolent Creator is working all things according to His purposes. And for our good. These subterfuges are no more than flimsy attempts to justify our rebellion.

The evidence is both clear and substantial, God exists. Many people want to deal with Him on their terms. God lovingly cannot allow that. Just as we now know, our parents loving authority was best for us, we will understand what God allows people to initiate on their own over time.

"Pain and suffering" a topic that cries out for sympathy and concern. When an unbeliever brings it up as a reason to disbelieve in God, we tend to identify with their experience. Our answers should never come across as perfunctory or casual. We must identify with them in their plight. Whether the pain is their own or someone else's, it is real, and we want our answer to be clothed in compassion.

Having acknowledged this, here is an answer:

Agreed that pain and suffering are grievous problems. The book *When Bad Things Happen to Good People* concluded that either God was good enough but didn't have the power, or had the power but wasn't good.

Not very encouraging.

Plus, if we do away with God, the pain and suffering are still there and now we are even worse off than before, but with no possible meaning attainable, and no hope. With God we have a basis for hope. Maybe He will answer our prayer? Or maybe there is a purpose, an eventual benefit. But with no God and no potential benefit, the suffering becomes pointless and meaningless—the worst kind.

When we were small children we might have had to endure a medical procedure. It was for our benefit, but we were too young to understand. But we understood pain!

If God is sovereign and good, then we have hope, a very good thing indeed. And if we have evidence that He is trustworthy as well as good, we are better equipped to handle whatever comes.

Just as with small children, who could not at that time understand the pain they had to endure would bring eventual benefit, we can make the decision that, in the face of the mountain of evidence pointing to God's certain existence, we can choose the position that, at this time, we do not know the "why" of suffering, but we can give God the benefit of the doubt. And later on, just as we now know and appreciate the "whys" of our childhood pain, God may inlighten us into that understanding also.

Pain and suffering comes to us all, sooner or later, including to those we love. Don't face it without hope.

The children are, for the most part, unprepared. We can change that by providing them with nontechnical, simple insights and easily transferrable concepts, from parent to child, and from student to student….things that are, upon reflection and examination, self-evident. Axiomatic.

Evolution gives children the false choice between "*theory and faith*" and most telling, between science and God. They use the prestige of science against the children and us, to fortify their claim. It is outrageous that these God-haters, (we must say it with tears) use the very science that in all aspects points to God, to make an argument against God! How long will they get away with it?

As far as I can tell, they offer no explanation of where the laws of physics came from, or how and why the laws rule and are so reliable. Search as you will and science offers no evidence for the origins of the Laws of Nature or Physics. They know that the very existence of LAWS points to a LAWGIVER....the very One they are fleeing from.

Science begins with the claim that nothing exists beyond the material, physical world. The *Oxford English Dictionary*, the most authoritative source in the English language, and some would say, in the world, defines science thus:

> "The intellectual and practical activity encompassing the systematic study of the structure and behavior of the physical and natural world through observation and experiment."

This definition excludes the existence of anything beyond the material world. There is no place for the transcendent, or supernatural. We have all supposed that their denial of God is because of something they have learned, or think they have learned, in their labs and studies. This is profoundly not true!

Their quest begins, at the very origin of the *theory* of evolution, with the attempt to find an explanation apart from God. They imagine vast stretches of time, billions of years. And further imagine a tooth fairy they call natural selection, something no one has ever seen. Then the biggest stretch of all, they think given enough time, this "blind, mindless and without purpose," entity, process, force, will create all we now see and experience!

At the inception, there was no science on the microscopic complexities of the cell. We now know the elements and the DNA of everything had to be created first. Think about it, can you believe *everything came from nothing.* How? *It helps if you are willing to park your brain at the door and believe anything the "experts" say. And you can wonder why they never offer the explanation why evolution is the better answer.*

CHAPTER

3

A (Covert) Declaration of War—On You!

Are you old enough to remember the 500th anniversary of Columbus Day the 12th of October 1992? Articles began to appear in various publications half a decade or so before the event. It was pointed out that the 400th anniversary, a century earlier in 1892, was celebrated border-to-border and coast-to-coast across the United States.

Because Americans love celebrations, with the vastly improved transportation and communications since 1892, we would have the celebration to top all others in our nation's history in 1992, the 500th anniversary.

However, a little later, other articles were published. For example, it was reported that Christopher Columbus was a Christian, and later on, it was reported that his diaries had never been translated into English. The last article I remember was that he was Jewish by birth, but had become a completed Jew through faith in Messiah Jesus!

Somewhere along the way the unfolding information proved to be the last straw. I have no memory of the 500th anniversary. Do you? I suppose the powers of darkness decided they would have no part in glorifying the Lord Jesus Christ. Devoid of funding and leadership, plans were shelved and the holiday came and went. Faith was, and still is, under attack.

The purpose of this chapter is to show you the power dark forces have to promote and conceal truth.

> *For we wrestle not against flesh and blood, but against principalities, against powers, against the rulers of the darkness of this world, against spiritual wickedness.* (Ephesians 6:12)

Here is how the enemy of God has opposed Biblical teachings. A new religion has been devised by the principalities and powers to oppose the Bible, God's Word. It is called Humanism. Humanism is a religion. It is a covert declaration of war on the church.

This appears on page 128 in the book *Humanism: A New Religion,* by Charles Francis Potter. My guess is not many Christians were aware of this declaration of war upon our children way back then.

©1930

Here's a direct quote from the book (page 128):

"Education is thus a most powerful ally of humanism, and every American public school is a school of humanism. What can the Theistic Sunday schools, meeting for an hour once a week, and teaching only a fraction of the children, do to stem the tide of a five-day program of humanistic teaching?"

Do you suppose anyone realized back in 1930 that Humanists had declared war on God, and His sons and daughters? Fighting a covert war gives advantage to the aggressor.

What kind of world does your family face?

A world of unbelievers who have been conditioned by the educational system, believes that science has all the answers, and that you and your Christian message are the enemy. When we put our kids into a poisonous secular environment without any preparation for the devious tactics of Satan, it is almost akin to human sacrifice. I know that sounds strong, but stick with me.

The new High Priests of Humanism are unbelieving scientists. You are told to believe what you are taught. Excommunication is the consequence in academia and many scientific circles for not being in lock step with this Godless *theory*. You resist at your peril.

We can teach the children that order in the universe points to purpose, intention, fruitfulness, and productivity—to the existence of a Creator. Each of these intrinsic truths point to a divine Mind, to God. They cohere and fit together, and when understood, are found to be self-evident. The enemy takes the Gospel, something that is beneficial and valuable to every individual and makes it seem like Bad News.

Evolution pontificates on things it knows nothing about, because the definition of science limits its world to the physical and natural. Evolutionists have no authority beyond that, by its own definition. But it doesn't stop them.

We must make our youth aware of the deception! This is why our children cannot understand us when we speak of spiritual things. They have been conditioned to believe that the natural world is all there is, and nothing exists beyond it. It makes absolutely no difference that there is no conceivable way to prove against an unseen world, but the enemy rejects the spiritual realm anyway.

The world thinks that the *theory* of evolution is fully validated and certified as the fullest expression of the triumph of modern science. "It's a hoax folks." Evolution is only a theory. It takes more faith to believe in evolution, literally that nothing created everything, than faith required to believe in God. Belief in God is rational, logical and rationally self-evident. It's axiomatic.

These insights in the book you're holding are practical, line up with our common experience and are self-evident. They will help children and adults with simple, nontechnical answers that reveal the deception we are being forced to believe.

At this point in your reading, you now know more than most Christians in the world about the nature of the conflict where our children are being cruelly brainwashed and intimidated by the *theory* of evolution.

4

The Fish Tank

I heard or read of an experiment involving a largemouth bass in a fish tank at a research lab. The tank had been fitted with slots so that a glass pane could be inserted dividing the tank into two separate compartments. In the beginning, the fish had the full range of the tank. When live minnows were put into the tank, the bass would pursue, catch and eat the minnows.

After a suitable time of conditioning, a glass pane was inserted creating two sections in the tank. The glass is transparent, not being detectable under the water. Those conducting the experiment allowed a period of time for the fish to adapt to the new, restricted limitations, and then put a minnow on the opposite side of the glass divider from the bass.

"Lunch," the bass thought, and not being aware of the glass sped forward only to hit the glass head-on. Ouch! Confusion sets in. The bass gives it a second try but this time a little more tentatively, so it did not hit the glass as hard this time around. Boom again! After repeated attempts, the fish gives up.

In his mind, that minnow is just not possible for him to capture and eat. And here's where it gets interesting. Those conducting the experiment removed the glass barrier, and the minnow swims freely around the fish. No response. It is as if the fish decided "that minnow is just not in the realm of possible lunch for me!"

Here's the point of the story. It's likely that many Christians, pastors, and denominations have given up on the battle against the faith-destroying and God-denying *theory* of evolution. And no wonder, we've had our heads handed back to us on a platter with every engagement.

Welcome to mind control.

A couple of generations ago, Christians who were also scientists, offered what has become known as Creation Science as an alternative to the *theory* of evolution. "You are trying to teach religion in the science classroom, and we won't stand for it," the secularists screamed!

Later on, others proposed the approach of Intelligent Design. Same result. Still later others proposed Specified Complexity as an argument for God and against evolution. Again, possibility thinking was castigated and defeated. Most recently the *theory* of Irreducible Complexity was shot down. So, it is no wonder that we cower before the *theory* of evolution. The defeats of the past still linger and still hurt.

If you can be persuaded that to go against evolution, is like saying you think you know more than the scientists, that, my friend, is checkmate!

Who can say that they know more than the scientists? You? Me? I don't think so. So, is it really then, checkmate? Are there any other cards to play? Let's switch metaphors. Instead of us being the confused and befuddled fish that has been conditioned to believe the minnow is unreachable, you are the minnow and evolution is the big fish. And your assignment is to take him down! Impossible! Impossible? Don't give up!

If you could have polled the troops when David faced Goliath, no one on Goliath's side would have bet on David. Probably the same if you had polled David's side. After all, what are the chances of a mere youth with next to no weaponry at all, coming up against the very latest in weaponry and armor and battle-tested championship expertise? None at all. Unless, as David testifies, "the battle is the Lord's!" In that case, any victory will be His victory, using mere shepherd's tools and tactics.

So, it is time for a new kind of warfare. Not so much against the establishment, so to speak, or about changing their minds on anything. Let us aim, rather for the minds and hearts of the people and the children. Insights that are offered in simple and nontechnical terms, and that are self-evident and easily grasped can be easily passed on. Can we deliver? Spectacularly, we believe. This is our aim. Read on.

5

The Origins of the *Theory* of Evolution

*The prime agenda of evolutionists is to destroy faith in God.
Science is the savior; you need no other.*
– The promise of evolution.

What can be learned by considering the origins of the *theory* of evolution? Well for one thing we can ask the "why" and the "who". Who were these people seeking to establish an alternate explanation for things that did away with the need for God? And what provoked it all?

Their excuses include hypocrisy in the church, sin in the church, (the crusades, the inquisition, selling indulgences). Natural disasters, like the Lisbon earthquake of 1755 where an estimated 60,000 men, women and children died, along with the Black Death plague jumped to their justification. The pain and suffering seen everywhere upon the innocent, is apparently also God's fault in their minds.

All these excuses played their part in the attempted

justification for the flight from God. The real reason was the rebellion in the heart of those who saw God not as the loving heavenly Father, but as a killjoy standing between them and their prideful natural inclinations.

Here is a quote from the evolution's founder, Charles Darwin in *The Origin of Species*:

> "I can indeed hardly see how anyone ought to wish Christianity to be true; for if so the plain language of the text seems to show that the men that do not believe, and this would include my father, brother, and all my best friends, will be everlastingly punished and this is a damnable doctrine."

And remember, Darwin could only see a cell with a primitive scope. A cell has a universe within it including DNA. Darwin did not know the macro and micro limits that exist in nature.

Do you see the implications? The founders of the *theory* of evolution resolutely and purposefully with full resolve and intent set out to find justification in doing away with God! That is not what we've been carefully taught. *The church and the world believe it was what they learned in their labs and fields of study that convinced them that evolution and natural selection were the true cause of all creation. (And they are all neutral, fair and unbiased, right?)*

Darwin's rejection of God and *theory* of evolution are not founded in scientific research, but in his personal rebellion against God. His decision was made at the very beginning. That is not at all what we have been led to believe. Consider...

- Where do evolutionists say everything came from? The Big Bang.
- Where does Evolution say the Big Bang came from? A Point of Singularity.
- Where does Evolution say the Point of Singularity came from? They don't say.
- Where does Evolution say the laws of nature come from? They don't say.
- Do they say why the laws are dependable? No.
- Do they say why the laws are knowable, discernible and comprehendible? No.

You are expected to just believe what they say, to trust them. You know, like taking candy from strangers. Or, shut up and drink the Kool-Aid.

Consider some of what the children face when they side against the evolution establishment. The schools pretty much succeed in convincing children that:

To believe in God is unscientific.
And superstitious.
And primitive.
And disputes and opposes science.
And, all valid science and scientists affirm evolution.
And all the evidence supports it.
And "your faith is not evidence".
Our *theory* is.
Now you will fall in line and accept our authority
Or face the ongoing consequences of:

Persecution.

Shunning.

Being slotted as religious,

and primitive,

and superstitious,

and poorly educated,

and hate filled,

unkind,

and unloving.

And with viewed with disdain.

The weapons to defeat evolution are not technical. They are easy to understand insights. They confirm experience and are self-evident. By this we mean that the insight makes sense and follows the rules of logic, and makes sense to us personally. Why should you trust strangers?

For example: Both science and common sense declare "NOTHING comes from nothing." Evolution offers no explanation of how it all got started. After all a Big Bang requires a Big Banger who lights the fuse. The Bible does explain. The explanation is God started it, which is both rational and plausible. The enemy replies "where did God come from?"

The answer is in two parts and is not complicated.

First, both reason and experience testify "everything that begins to exist has a cause." We know and experience the physical world, so we know *something exists*. We know something caused it. Second, there must be by necessity an "uncaused first cause." Call it what you will. I call it God. Unless you are fleeing from God, this is a reasonable, rational, satisfying and common-sense conclusion.

The other side doesn't want a God. After all, he would have to be personal, because for humans to be personal and have personality, it would, by necessity have to issue forth from a "person." Nothing else would make sense.

So, evolutionists reason, a personal God probably has a moral code He would expect us to live by it; and to them, that is NOT good news. This is a liberating insight revealing why the theory of evolution exists. In fact, flight from God is the only reason for evolution. This is clear from its origins. This is the plausible reason why they flee from God.

The argument for evolution is appealing only if the idea of God is bad news. Apart from that, evolution will not hold up to even rudimentary questions or examination. For example, if the idea of God were not so distasteful, one might wonder what criteria were used in making the determination of the cause being (A) Evolution, and not (B) God. Where could we could go to examine the criteria for ourselves? Another essential part is our perception is that we perceived the scientists as neutral, as trustworthy and reliable, as unbiased and not having an unspoken, or hidden agenda. A look at the origins of the theory explodes that lie.

The theory of evolution is a search for an explanation for creation other than considering God. If one is eager to believe against God, he might not require the same level of proof to reach a conclusion he favors, as he would to accept one he views as to his disadvantage. This is the advantage every "con-man" enjoys.

As Christians we are under obligation to live our lives in

ways that do not give unbelievers a reason to doubt the goodness of God.

Atheists are people of great faith. They believe in politics, not "In God we trust," but "In government we trust!" Not having any other option, they are forced to put their trust in government What a sad and unpromising hope!

They naively have no choice but to believe bureaucrats and politicians will handle their positions of trust with integrity and trustworthiness against all the evidence compiled revealing the fallenness of human nature.

They realize all humanity faces temptation and when government officials are tempted, not knowing God is keeping score, will seek a rational basis to succeed in resisting the temptation. Otherwise, the voters may lose faith in the system, the government will go broke, and we will face collapse and anarchy. Keep the faith. Trust government! Who needs God anyhow!

What if banishing God in the classroom equates, with "we are not made in God's image," therefore we lose some of our meaning, dignity, significance, purpose and value? I am inclined to believe that put this way, a considerable majority would favor allowing God back into the classroom. The objectors might be somewhat pacified with a generic "god," but not Christian, Jewish or Muslim. Evolutionists just want some authority figure who conveys value to all persons. That is not science, shout objectors! Really? Who gave them the authority to decide what is and what is not, science?

Scientists who proclaim, "faith in God is not scientific" are talking out of turn. Their authority to speak is limited to the physical and natural world. Think about it! Anything existing beyond the physical is beyond scope of their area of expertise. Their position is no more than speculation and conjecture no matter how much they fume and fuss. Speaking practically, faith in evolution is not science.

Could it be possible? Is there even a one in a million chance that what they have proclaimed about the theory of evolution is not the whole story? Is it possible that evolution is really no more than an alternate explanation that leaves God out? And can it be proved? And haven't we been told that religion is only a holdover from pre-scientific times and that faith is not different from superstition, myth, fable and fairytales and legends? Evolutionists say modern well-educated people no longer look for, look to God? Why would anyone question them? Doesn't evolution answer all the questions? Are there other vital considerations left out? What, for instance?

Evolution – the greatest lie ever sold!

The goal is to answer the questions and to send our children out into the world informed….armored, unafraid, bold and confident.

The goal is to provide insights that are not technical, but are easy to understand and defeat the evolution juggernaut. (Someone made the term Big Pharma a well-known pejorative. Can we add Big Science?)

It is science that claims, without any basis or supporting evidence, the authority to pontificate and rule not only in their field, but also beyond and into metaphysics, the spiritual and to the existence or non-existence of God. Tell the children how the science establishment came to the conclusion against God. It was not from what they learned in science.

Tell us explicitly WHAT it was that weighed against God? After all, don't they represent there are millions of tons of evidence? Your children think what their authority figures learned from science made them atheists.

What the authority figures learned was dogma and not science.

6

Probability of Evolution Occurring

Let's consider how the evolutionists guess at how life first came into being. They suppose that billions of years ago lightning (wonder where lightning comes from?) struck a *primordial nutrient rich swamp,* (wonder where the swamp or a *primordial soup* came from?) and produced the first primitive life form. Or, a big bang exploded and threw together nothing to create order out of everything that exists in the known universe.

And consider evolutionists eliminate the possibility of design, but surmise a random process with no intellect caused the creation of all we observe on earth. Let's look at the probability of a random combination of sequential events needed to successfully create life, as we observe it, and you judge whether evolution could possibly be a scientific fact or just a theory.

*Definition of **probability***
prob·a·bil·i·ty
1: the quality or state of being **probable**

2: something (such as an event or circumstance) that is probable

3a (1): the ratio of the number of outcomes in an exhaustive set of equally likely outcomes that produce a given event to the total number of possible outcomes

3a (2): the chance that a given event will occur

So, what is the probability of the process of evolution successfully occurring for human life to exist? Here is an example of how to calculate probability, when tossing two coins to determine the maximum number of combinations you can realize.

For 2 coins tossed, there are four possibilities: heads–heads, heads-tails, tails- heads, and tails-tails. That is 4 possibilities. To determine the total number of possibilities for any combination of coins, we simply multiply the number of coins tossed by the number of sides (two) as follows:

2 sides for 1 coin equals 2 possibilities
2 sides each for 2 coins equals 4 possibilities (shown above)
2 sides each for 3 coins equal 8 possibilities
2 sides each for 4 coins equal 16 possibilities

So step one, has a possibility of one in two. Step two has a possibility of one in four. And step three has a possibility of one in eight, and step four, one in sixteen. Each succeeding step doubles the possibility of the preceding step. The greater number of stages of complexity, the lower the chances of successful results occurring. What are the chances of winning the lottery? A few ping pong balls, and you have a million to one chances of winning.

Note with twenty coin tosses the probability of successfully choosing a correct number is over a million to one. (The odds of getting twenty "heads" in a row.) That means only twenty steps (coin tosses) in creating life would require a million sequential steps. But, that does not take into account the millions of steps needed, and the creation of various independent body parts that had to evolve without a functional purpose. Consider the necessary parts of our hearing mechanism, or eye components, evolving out of nowhere to create a working eye that sees or ear that hears!

Note with only thirty-coin tosses, the probability of successfully choosing a correct number is over 1 billion to 1. Consider that scientists believe the earth is 4.5 billion years old. That means a successful step in the evolutionary process has to occur every 4.5 years. What? The complexity of a human being is much greater that thirty consecutive events! If you cut yourself with something sharp, there are some twenty-five consecutive chemical events that have to occur to stop the blood from bleeding out. One step missing and you bleed to death.

Forty steps (tosses) require 1,099,811,627,776 steps. Almost two trillion simple steps (there are only 2 sides to a coin). That means each consecutive step would have to occur in less than 4.5 billion years divided by 1099 billion steps. That's 0.0045 years or 1.6425 days.

I can believe some of these scientists' brains were created in 1.6425 days, but I can't see randomly placing the head of a man in 1.6425 days on his shoulders rather than on his hips, or more than two eyes in his head (why not 10) instead of all around his waist. Folks you have 1.6425 days per step.

How did the reproductive system get created?

And where did the man-women models come from?

Probability Theory

If someone says "There will be a car crash on your street tomorrow," there are a wide range of possibilities, based on circumstances to consider. Do you live on a major arterial or a quiet neighborhood street? Does your "street" run a long distance or only one block? Are there many residents, visitors, delivery vehicles and municipal service vehicles, or only a few? And so on. All of these will enter into the calculation of whether or not a crash is "likely or probable." (Probability *theory.*)

Possibility Theory

STEP ONE: Possibility *theory* is different. Either the crash will happen tomorrow, or it won't with a 50/50 chance. The predictor has a one chance in two of being right.

STEP TWO: What happens when you add a second contingency? What if we say, "one of the vehicles will be a black car?" You have doubled the contingencies. Number one, either the crash will happen, a one in two chance, or it will not. And the additional condition, one will be a black car makes it a one in two chance, if the only colors were black and white. So, the likelihood of the crash occurring (1) and that one of the cars will be black (2) is one in four.

STEP THREE: Let's add a third contingency. (3) "one of the drivers will be a woman." The chance that the crash will occur, and one of the cars will be black, and one of the drivers will be a woman is one in eight. As we add more contingencies, each stage

50

doubles with each success.

Consider the evolutionists belief of how life first came into being. They suppose that billions of years ago lightning (wonder where lightning comes from?) struck a "primordial nutrient rich swamp," (wonder where the swamp came from, and where all that 'primordial soup' came from?) producing the first primitive life form.

What would be the most basic life form you could conceive of? It would have to be one which at least had the ability to (1) find food, the ability to (2) catch or harvest the food, the ability to (3) eat the food, the ability to (4) digest the food, the ability to (5) convert the food to energy and the (6) the ability to circulate it to the individual cells, or body parts. And, (7) it would need the ability to collect waste from the cells and the ability to transport it to a place to excrete it, and (8) the ability to reproduce itself and the offspring would have to be able to accomplish all the above, and so on down the line. And along the way begin to "evolve" upward, against everything the scientists have found regarding the 2nd Law of Thermodynamics, which we will discuss in a later chapter.

What are the odds?

1) To find food.. 1 in 2
2) To catch the food 1in 4
3) To digest the food .... 1 in 8
4) To distribute the food........................ 1 in 16
5) The ability of cells to process............. 1 in 32
6) The ability of cells to process waste... 1 in 64
7) The ability to move waste................... 1 in 128
8) The ability to excrete waste .... 1 in 256

9) The ability to meet a partner............. 1 in 512
10) The ability to reproduce.................... 1 in 1024

Of course, this is only a partial list. How many more essential parts and functions might there be? You have to double only twenty times to exceed one million, and 21 times would be two million, 22 times – four million, and a second doubling that would be only 40 in number produces an astronomical number that I don't even know how to write! And should we double the numbers for each of the eight million+ species that are living today?

Critical Thinking

Developing critical-thinking skills is easier than you think!

The range of the study of critical thinking is so comprehensive that you could devote your life to it. This does not mean, however, that you cannot learn some things with minimum commitment.

Skimming over the waves, for example, we can learn that critical thinking involves things like paying attention to what is being said, and questioning….ask lots of questions.

Train ourselves to ask: "If this proposition is true, what necessarily follows?" And, "Are there other factors to be considered that are all common sense in their nature?"

For example, the statement may be made: "Highly educated and credentialed people who have devoted their lives in the pursuit of science have concluded there is no God!"

At this point we can go in the direction of various pursuits: "Really?" "Do you suppose they have looked everywhere?" And so on. You may want to save that line of inquiry for later.

Right now, let's raise the question: "If 'A' is true, what necessarily follows?"

If there is no God, then laws are only man made, and only reflect someone's opinion. Why wouldn't it be okay to conclude that "You can make rules for you – and I'll make rules for me?" And "mind your own business!" Sounds like a plan for chaos.

Moving along, we are forced to make some very questionable conclusions. If there is no God, then: Nothing created everything! That doesn't sound very right. How could that be? And:

Non-Life Created Life! ....That's not too promising either.

Chaos Created Order! .... It's getting farther and farther from experience and from common sense!

Non-Consciousness Created Consciousness! ....It's hard to visualize how that could be.

Non-Personal Created Personal! .. You'll need to explain that one.

Non-Rational Created Rational! ....Ditto.

Blind Created Vision!........................... Surely there is abundant evidence to prove all this?

Deaf Created Hearing! ....Yeah, I'm beginning to get the idea.

There's more. But normally you are given only two choices, God, or Natural Selection. The promoters of Natural Selection insist everything was created by a *something blind and mindless and without purpose or intention.* They are forced into that most untenable position in order to keep their opponents from saying "Natural Selection is just your name for God!"

The world demonstrates a very great degree of order and organization, of great diversity and complexity, of productivity and fruitfulness, of dependability and predictability, of intelligibility and know-ability. Do these things correspond with a *Mind*? The answer is self-evident.

People are ready to believe these unlikely things because the god they have imagined is to be avoided at all cost. Jesus was kind, merciful, generous and just and a whole lot of other positive things. It is some caricature of God they reject, not the Jesus of the New Testament. If they knew Him like you know Him, they would love Him like you love Him!

7

How an Event in A.D.70 Demolishes "Higher Criticism" of the New Testament

Modern scholarship, so called, has cast serious doubt on the validity and the reliability of the New Testament record. It is asserted by some that the New Testament documents are not eyewitness accounts by reliable contemporary witnesses who were recording what they had seen and heard and experienced.

Rather, these critics having so-called impressive credentials, have carefully examined many writings from that era, and decisively conclude that the New Testament records were written much later than when the events actually occurred, probably a hundred, or perhaps hundreds of years later. And they are found to exhibit characteristics of legends and fables rather than the actual factual accounts they claim to be.

The world and much of the church have bowed to this "superior" scholarship. We don't have the training or knowledge of these so-called scholars, so who are we to question? What can we do? Are there signs of authenticity for the NT that you do not have to be a scholar to know with certainty? Let's see.

It is an undisputed fact of history that in A.D.70 the Roman army destroyed Jerusalem and the temple. The temple was far more central to the lives of the people of that day than the twin towers of the World Trade Center (WTC) and the events of 9/11 ever were to most of us.

What if you ran across a travel brochure in an old magazine regarding the WTC, and reading it learned that it had its own zip code, and told how many people worked there, how many visitors came on a typical day, and other interesting data? Let's say you read to the end and there was no mention of 9/11 and the destruction of the towers. How can we explain that? Would you agree that the most reasonable explanation would be that the document was written before the event?

It is an important and self-evident fact that the New Testament makes no mention of the destruction of the temple. If the records had been written after this, they likely would have included the account of the destruction of the temple. It would have verified and embellished Jesus' credentials as a prophet (Matthew 24:2, Mark 13:2, Luke 21:6-7).

What is the answer? Why no mention? Isn't the most likely explanation why the New Testament does not mention the destruction of the temple is that the New Testament documents were already written, had been copied probably many times, and were being circulated throughout the region as the book of Acts testifies?

ACTS 8:1 tells that after the martyrdom of Stephen a great

persecution rose against the church and all believers except the apostles left Jerusalem. This was a large number of people. Remember, 3,000 were added to the church at Pentecost, and more multitudes later. These were scattered abroad and took their personal experiences and their written accounts with them.

Though millions have been deceived by the "scholarship" and the "expertise" of the enemies of God that deny the New Testament reliability, the events of A.D.70 refute them and prove the *scholarship* to be false. This is conclusive and adequate proof of the validity of the New Testament documents. These insights destroy the critic's bogus claim of *scholarship*! The world and the church can understand this. And you don't have to trust anyone. The facts are self-evident, and in line with both common sense and with experience.

Your children can understand this. We can arm them to withstand the assault they face every day in school. Let's save the world, one child at a time. And when enough third graders understand, look for a third-grade awakening!

Review and Reflect

The destruction of Jerusalem and the temple in AD70 is an undisputed fact of history.

The absence of any mention of it in the 259 chapters of the New Testament is verifiable to anyone taking the time to check for themselves.

These two certainties demolish the conclusions of the *scholars* who want to deny the authentic, contemporaneous, and eye witness character of the New Testament documents.

You have by these two facts established the reliability of

God's record of the events. This means you can safely put your trust in what God has recorded in scripture. The *evidence* against the New Testament is revealed to be a sham. Like evolution it is revealed to be pseudo-science. It is only, and no more than, a duplicitous attempt to explain everything apart from God.

Now you can be certain of it. Put your trust in the Lord. The evidence for God is overwhelming. Jesus' testimony, by these truths validated, declare the accurate historic Genesis account, complete with Adam and Eve, and the six-day creation, and Noah's flood, as well as the reliability and dependability of all of scripture. What a firm foundation for our bold and confidant witness to a world in darkness!

8

What We Don't Know Doesn't Have to Defeat Us

When you think about it, what we don't know is much greater than what we do know. So, when scientists present the theory of evolution to you, and they tell you it is science, and if you don't go along, you are in effect saying that you are smarter than scientists. The pressure is on.

This is where the liberal churches find themselves. They realize the case is being made by those with impressive credentials, and that church people are not trained to challenge scientific claims. Therefore, they cave and go along with the faux science on evolution, and try to salvage as much of the gospel as they can.

After a century of compromise and capitulation, there is not much of the gospel left. And not many "liberal" churches either. How about you? Do you have the credentials to question what many scientists insist are the valid answers to the questions of origins?

As a mental exercise put your palms together with hands

out stretched; now open so your hands are extended to either side. Let this represent how much we know. Now move your hands to the rear, behind your back. Let this represent how much we do not know. Now, in all that we do not know, it can be tempting to wonder if the God-denying scientists are right. Would we, (we wonder) believe just like the scientists if we knew as much as they do? Good question.

The answer is no one knows everything. But we can analyze what we do know and come to a conclusion. Let's try. So, what do we do? Do we agree that only the men in the white lab coats have the authority to tell us what to think? I don't think so!

Yogi Berra famously said: "You can observe a lot by just looking!" When my granddaughter was small she enjoyed telling me the way to eat an elephant. One bite at a time! Can we break it down into bite sizes? Philosophers generally agree the first question is "why is there something rather than nothing?" You and I can go out into the world and, without the help of someone in a white lab coat, learn some basic things without their assistance. Let's see if we can decide for ourselves what makes sense and what is absurd conjecture and speculation.

Here's a brief review and reiteration:

First, everywhere we look the world exhibits a great deal of order and of organization. What or who produced that complexity: God or something else?

Second, adding to the order and organization, we find an enormous diversity of things, and all having great complexity. Wonder why? God, or something else?

Third, to the order and organization, and the complexity and diversity, we find fruitfulness and productivity. Why would that be? God, or something else?

Fourth, with the order and organization, the diversity and complexity, along with the fruitfulness and productivity, we find a measure of inter-relatedness and inter-dependability. Why should it be so? God, or something else?

Fifth, there is a reliability and dependability in the system of things. Water always boils at 212 degrees Fahrenheit at sea level everywhere and always. Wonder why? God, or something else?

Sixth, there is predictably in everything we can observe. God or something else?

Seventh, the dependability and predictability point to a set of laws that govern globally. Wonder why? God, or something else?

Eighth, the most remarkable discovery of all is that these Laws are intelligible, discoverable and knowable! Why? How can this be?

It is explainable in one of two ways. It is the result of a big explosion in space and nothing else, or from God.

Now, if you have no agenda to do away with God, it is an easy step to conclude that it is all a result of an Intelligent, Purposeful, Infinite and Personal Being…God, the God of the Bible.

That is not much of a stretch at all. However, if your view of God is so terrible then you will grasp at any straw, believe any absurdity, and take any risk to avoid that terrible outcome, you need to come up with an alternate explanation. Precisely what the *theory* of evolution purports to be. And the only reason to believe, the only need for the *theory* - is to escape God!

Have mercy on them. Pray for them. And do everything you can to destroy confidence in the *theory* of evolution!

Review and Reflect

The very scientists who deny the existence of anything beyond the physical and material, even though there is no conceivable way to test or to prove it, still have the temerity to pontificate to us against God! They may have a measure of persuasive success inside the bounds of their guilds, but not with us. Scientists normally say they are limited to the physical and natural. Beyond that, as modern science and technology testifies, they choose to ignore the truth manifested in all creation.

All the evidence points to God. Don't you know that if they had a shred of proof or any evidence against God, they wouldn't be able to shut up about it. You are wise to question their pronouncements.

9

The Origins of the Laws of Physics

Have you ever wondered why the evolutionists never offer any insights or explanations on the origins of the laws of physics? The rule, authority, regularity, and dependability of the laws of physics are the foundation of science and modern technology.

Why do the laws exist? Where do they come from? From whence comes their power to enforce their jurisdiction over everything? Why are they knowable and predictable? What is the source of their authority?

Evolutionists address none of these. But I believe they know. They have to know. Their rebellion is a conscious and deliberate one. Laws are necessary to formulate theories and to test, verify or falsify them. You couldn't even formulate a *theory*, much less verify or falsify it without laws. The laws limit what will and what will not work.

A few hundred years ago Isaac Newton saw apples fall from a tree and deduced the law of gravity. Other scientists who were household names a few generations ago, before the enemy seized control of the schools, began to discern regularity in nature, and discovered and formulated other laws. The Periodic Table of the elements was conceived and began to take shape and reveal order in the material world.

Many elements were abundant in nature and their atomic weights and numbers began the classifications. As the years went on, other elements were discovered and filled the gaps. Some very rare elements were missing in the table, but anticipated, until finally the table was complete with no gaps and no missing spaces. Order and organization, like everything else, point to a creator—God.

Over the decades and centuries, many other discoveries added to what we now take for granted as *The Laws of Physics*. These laws of physics are the basis for the prestige of modern science. This prestige is a major reason for the success of the God-denying *theory* of evolution. We enjoy what modern science provides—photography of man's footprints on the moon, air conditioning, automobiles, and the internet.

Can you see how these achievements are a powerful incentive for the layman to believe whatever scientists say concerning evolution is true? And when those scientists take the position the unseen God is not the answer for the origins of man, we are not inclined to argue with their *authority*.

However, laws infer or imply a Lawgiver. The Lawgiver is who the evolutionists are fleeing from. They offer no *theory* of the origins of the laws of physics because there is no plausible explanation that could attribute the laws to a big explosion in space. And the Big Bang is their best substitute for God. For them, it's the only game in town.

Why not use logic to compare the possibilities of all of creation designed by a creator with incontrovertible, unchangeable laws versus an explosion of chaos that created order and scores of predictable standards by accident.

There is a reason why the laws are reliable, repeatable, and dependable. Chaos creates chaos, not order. There is a reason why laws rule as a standard. Otherwise, why would scientists search for order if the rules were ever changing? There is a reason and intentionality, a purpose why the laws of physics are intelligible and are comprehendible. There isn't a single creation of mankind that is not based on dependable laws of science. The reason is God.

Scientists do not throw items at a wall and expect to create a battery-operated car.

I haven't found anything from the evolutionists regarding the origins of the laws of physics. They don't offer an explanation of why they exist. I think they fear that the whole idea of *laws point to the Lawgiver*...the very One they are trying to do away with. So, they remain quiet and hope we don't notice.

The reason: rationality, intentionality, purpose, and intelligibility are the product of a Divine Mind. Evolutionists maintain that their source of all creation is natural selection, which Richard Dawkins' defines as "blind, mindless and without purpose." This requires credulity, sometimes called "parking your brain at the door." Let's call it blind faith – the very thing they disparage Christians for! If anyone in the science guild has challenged Dawkins' dictate, they have been pretty quiet about it. Silence most often implies agreement, or, maybe in this case, fear of reprisal.

Come on… to deny the Originator of the laws of nature as a brilliant Mind, and to insist its origin is instead a blind, mindless and without-purpose force is laughable! …unless you fear or hate God. The Creator's mind is personal and the source of our personhood. This is self-evident.

Otherwise, you have the problem of how the *impersonal* created the *personal*. The reason is God.

It is self-evident from the science of ecology, that everything fits in and has a purpose in the overall scheme of things. If everything else has purpose, then so do we—dignity, significance, value, and meaning. All anchored in God, those attributes are self-evident – unless you reject God as bad news. And now you know why God is good news, and why evolutionists hate revealing the origins of the laws of physics.

Review and Reflect

All of modern science and technology rely on the dependability of the laws of physics. The evolutionists owe us an explanation of the origins of the laws. Since they have not given one, we are left to speculate that it is because their bankruptcy of *truth* provides no answer. Well, one reason they haven't needed to answer the origin question is because they employee intimidation and censorship tactics. It seems evolutionists find the existence of God *bad news* and limiting. We need to help the children see the real motive of this contrived lie. Ask yourself "Should I trust God, or an explosion based on speculation for the origins of these laws and my very being?"

——— 10 ———

Modern Science is Western Science

Wonder why that is? There is a reason. The Chinese invented gun powder. The Arabs delivered us from Roman Numerals. And, for the most part, the rest of modern science came out of Medieval Europe, in the late middle ages.

I took a class where the professor enjoyed talking about an experience from a previous class. "I told them to write their answers and number them with Arabic numerals." He enjoyed telling how one student wrote "I am using Roman Numerals because I don't know how to do Arabic numerals."

Here, from the *Oxford English Dictionary*, is their definition:

Arabic numeral

Noun: any of the numerals 0, 1, 2, 3, 4, 5, 6, 7, 8, and 9. Arabic numerals reached Western Europe (replacing Roman numerals) through Arabia by about A.D. 1200 but probably originated in India.

In that era Europe was called Christendom because the faith was widespread, and it was the dominant world view. The scientists had a common belief that a rational God would create a rational world. They set about to "think God's thoughts after Him," according to Johannes Kepler, scientist and mathematician, 1571 - 1630 A.D. This quest to find the rationality that God put into the world could never have risen out of:

Pantheism or any "local" gods' concept.
Or the idea that all is an illusion.
Or Hinduism that embraces the idea of millions of gods.
Or Buddhism that teaches that the world IS god.
Or from the evolutionary view that the "blind, mindless and non-purposeful"...process created everything.

It was the accepted rationality of *God* that was the foundational starting point of modern science!

The reason that modern science is Western science is the gospel of Jesus Christ, had swept Europe. The New Testament records establish the divinity of Jesus. Each book in the New Testament claims its authority not on the death, but on the resurrection of Jesus, the personal, powerful, healing, forgiving, and death-conquering Son of God, Deity.

Europe was called Christendom because the Gospel reigned there. It was believed by the scientists that a rational God would create a rational world.

This changes everything when you are asking the WHY questions. It explains the universality of the laws of physics. It explains their consistency and dependability. It explains their know-ability, and intelligibility, and discoverability. It explains their dense, deep information, all of which correspond with God, and not with a "blind, mindless and purposeless" process, which again is how Dawkins describes *natural selection*. The rules and knowledge contained in the laws are discoverable with sufficient research. This research would result in modern technology.

In 1967 the National Cash Register Company, ranked about 97th in size of the companies in the United States. They had an annual budget in research and development of $26 million dollars—a million dollars invested every two weeks. When you add the research and development investments of the larger companies, and the aggregate investments of more than half a century since, it tells us how dense the information is and the secrets are. Billions invested have given us modern technology.

Why are the laws of physics so dense with information and data? How did it get there? Why is it discernible, intelligible, and attainable? If you don't like the God answer, you will need substantial faith to go along with the answer of the evolutionists. They offer no answer.

The *theory* of evolution has no answers to this. Or rather, the answer of God is not acceptable to them and they hope the rest of us don't notice. They prefer to credit a random explosion! Don't try that at home!

They know that most everyone acquainted with computers knows the phrase GIGO or "garbage in, garbage out," referring to programming and data input. The integrity of the data and information contained in the laws of physics settles the question (unless you are fleeing) of *who* put the data in and *who* created mankind in a form so that they could be equipped to decipher.

If the existence of God is your worst nightmare you will go to any extreme and accept any absurdity to avoid God, such as, "nothing creating everything." *(That is a powerful insight.)*

Modern science and modern technology depend on the laws of physics and their reliability, dependability, intelligibility and discoverability. This is the foundation of the prestige of the scientists who turn around and use their prestige to destroy awareness of the One that made it all possible. They are enemies of God. Pray for them.

Review and Reflect

How deep is the resolve of evolutionists who know the true deficiencies of their standards?

The Watermelon Seed

The typical watermelon weighs approximately 145,000 times as much as the typical watermelon seed. (My granddaughter Addison researched this.) The seed looks dry and unimpressive. There is no indication that within it lies enormous power and potential. There is no indication that, even after a long time on the shelf, or in the seed store, that under the influence of soil, moisture, and sunshine something wakes up inside.

The watermelon's DNA provides enabling power to bring into existence a root thinner than a thread. (Similar seeds from acorns begin slender but can grow strong enough to put cracks in a concrete sidewalk, destroy the foundation of a house, or break up a roadway.) Within the seed is the ability and power to break the tough outer shell. Something provides motive-power to push through the soil to seek and find water, and to transport the water back to the seed. And then that something distributes to its component parts, which have the ability to use it to accomplish each part's individual task in building the vine and the resulting watermelon.

This takes energy—power. Where does this come from? God, unless you have a better answer.

Inside the tiny seed, alongside the DNA, which contains the instructions of the "how-to," is an energy source that provides the necessary power. And it would seem, there is also a manager or boss or something to supervise and see that everything is accomplished in the proper sequence, timetable and order...and in the proper proportion.

The seed uses the moisture to build a factory to extend the root system, and builds a vine that may extend 15 to 20 feet or more. In addition to having the power to build the vine, it finds the energy to transport back from deep in the soil, the moisture it needs to build the vine, and the leaves and the fruit.

The vine will grow many leaves, each with the remarkable ability to capture the sunshine and through an amazing and complex process of photosynthesis, create power to build a watermelon. Not just one, but perhaps a dozen or more on each vine. It will have the power and the know-how to draw adequate moisture to build something about 145,000 times its own weight...and to do it multiple times along that 15 to 20-foot vine.

It will put the moisture through a process of making sugar, delicious flavor, and find ways to make the green for the outside, red and white for the inside. And inside each watermelon, scattered around in the delicious red texture, are dozens of new seeds, each programmed with the potential to go out and do it again!

From whence comes this most phenomenal ability?

There are two contending views:

1. Most of the scientific world insists that there is no God and the truth is that this watermelon process is the result of *natural selection*. A previously-mentioned, prominent spokesman, Sir Richard Dawkins, describes *natural selection* as "blind, mindless and without purpose."

2. If it seems more likely to you that it would come from a purposeful intellect, that it would come from a Mind, then you must be one not desperately fleeing from a God, who you think is inconvenient.

Review and Reflect

You are given the opportunity of thinking for yourself, or letting someone else do your thinking for you. It is a high-stakes decision. Agree? And now you can help others.

—— 12 ——

Footprints on the Moon

There is more on the internet about the Lunar Lander than you would ever want to read. The part I found most interesting was the "how-to," the explaining, and assigning of the task.

"You are to build an aircraft that will operate in a zero atmosphere."

The next line was what got me. "The problem was solved in typical engineering fashion. We broke the larger problem down into as many small problems as we could. Then when all the smaller problems were solved, we had the Lunar Lander!"

This success resulted from *science*, in that the mission was a success and the crew returned safely. Science is possible because the laws of physics exist, and allow and limit according to their jurisdiction and power. They are reliable and dependable. Build an automobile this way and it will run, and so on. Follow the laws of aerodynamics and one can build a jet and have predictable outcomes.

When there are disasters, we learn something and future missions are safer because of what was learned. These dependable and reliable laws of physics are what make science possible. Yet, I have found no explanation from evolution science of the origins of the laws. Or why they rule. Or why they should be understandable and intelligible to us. A big explosion in space is not likely to produce an answer to their origin. Laws point to a Lawgiver. Perhaps that is why evolutionists are silent on this subject.

You've seen photos of the Lunar Lander, and of man's footprints on the moon. This describes a curious blend of science and of superstition.

The "superstition" involves the supposed great ages of the cosmos. The *theory* of evolution requires great swatches of time. Evolution supposedly occurs very slowly, so slow in fact that it cannot be observed. The replacement and substitution of God with the activating cause of natural selection is foundational in the flight from God.

It is imperative that billions of years must be involved and have elapsed since the big bang. Anything less and the *theory* will then collapse under its own weight. The supposed eons of time are believed because of various dating methods. Carbon dating is one of the most familiar. It measures the rate of radioactive decay within a rock, or a fossil and determines how long it will take to complete the transition. (This assumes, of course, that the "clock in the rock" began its countdown from zero, or from 100%. There is no scientific way to know this. And there is certainly no way to prove it.) Call it what it is, a faith position.

From this we calculate how long the transition has been going on. A less familiar dating method is the science of the measurement of the accumulation of dust from space. We have over a hundred years of data on space dust.

Since the scientists "knew" that the moon was at least (what?) millions, maybe billions of years old, they calculated the moons lower gravitation, and the fact of it having no atmosphere, and built the Lunar Lander with the legs several feet high or long. You have seen photos or video of the astronauts descending the ladder. This was consistent with the depth of dust that would have accumulated over the millions or billions of years.

Funny, the spectacular photography of man's footprints on the moon reveals a dust of accumulation consistent with an age of six to ten thousand years!

When scientists attempt to ascertain the age of the earth, some things are provable, some not. We can know with a high degree of certainty the RATE at which the process is occurring.

What we cannot know is that the "clock in the rock" began its countdown at zero.

Since this is not knowable, it is not science. Rather, it is speculative superstition. Not provable or verifiable scientifically, but believed without proof or evidence by evolutionists. Amazingly, it constitutes the foundational basis for the validity of the *theory* of evolution!

Evolutionists now realize that. So, they returned to their calculations and made the necessary adjustments and continued in their long war against God. And the public remained in the dark! Facts don't matter if your flight from God is desperate.

The supposed billions of years that scientists claim "prove" against the Bible, and against faith in God, and the basis to hold Christians in scorn are disproven by the photography of man's footprints on the moon.

You may not be qualified to refute their dating methods, their calculations, and their assumptions, because everyone not having personal expertise must "take it on faith." But you don't need to. You have seen the photographs. You can rest in the assurance that God is the better answer in the question of origins.

Man's footprints on the moon destroy the eon's long explanation of the cosmos. And establishes, for all to see that God is sovereign and He loves us. Good News. That is what the word Gospel means.

Review and Reflect

Pharaoh and his army were held back in the pursuit of Israel by the pillow of fire and the pillow of smoke. In spite of witnessing these supernatural phenomena, the (unbelieving) Egyptians still followed Moses and were drowned in the sea.

And despite having the curtain in the temple torn from top to bottom, and despite Jesus' resurrection from the dead –most of the Jewish religious leaders of that day refused to believe. (Thinking of Nicodemus, Joseph of Arimathea, and Paul as exceptions.)

And did the evolutionists repent upon the indisputable witness of the photography of men's footprints on the moon? Sadly, no. Their *will* to disbelieve is resolute. When you are convinced that God is bad news, for preferential purposes, you are forced to believe He does not exist. Evolution is the only game in town if you are fleeing God!

What Explains the Widespread Belief in Evolution?

Have you ever given any thought to why the teachers are so confident in their presentation of the *theory* of evolution as the explanation behind the entire Cosmos? They do not seem to leave much room for creative discourse. And the unarmed children are unequipped and helpless.

The children believe evolution because it is what they were taught. Their authority figures taught from the textbooks provided, that evolution confidently and authoritatively answers all questions about origins. And they sneak in metaphysical things as well, which are, of course not observable, repeatable or capable of being verified by an independent third party. This, by definition, renders it beyond the teachers and scientists qualifications and jurisdiction.

What needs to be brought into focus is why this is so. The answer is that the teachers themselves were confidently and authoritatively taught that by others.

And their teachers had the same experience, and so on, back up the line. Why is this important? Because it reveals that almost no one believes evolution based on their personal experience, but rather it is based on what they were taught by others. In other words, they believe evolution by faith!

And it is likely that as each generation was taught, there was the implied threat that if you don't go along, you will be seen as raising yourself above the collective experience and wisdom of all the scientists who have brought us this glorious and liberating discovery that delivers us from the tyranny of evil and malicious false gods. This is a look back trying to understand how such a mendacious *theory*, that is both God-denying and faith-destroying, could come to the dominance we see today.

At present the success of the selling of the *theory* is largely because the science community is seen as trustworthy, objective, neutral, fair, open-minded, and not having an agenda of their own. I believe the clear, discernable evidence shows this is not true.

How curious that their very starting point is that nothing exists beyond the physical, a starting point that at the beginning, before any investigation, without any foundation in science, insists that the spiritual and the transcendent do not exist! They maintain this arrogant posture without a shred of evidence, and without any possible way to prove it. They mask their agenda so effectively that their pose of objectivity is widely believed...or swallowed, which brings us to the next point.

The principal reason evolution is welcomed is that God is often perceived bad news! At least God, the way He is pictured, is bad news. Evolution is the devil's gospel, his good news. "There is no Deity judging you or forbidding you the things you enjoy most." There is no one making rules either. All rules are man-made and are therefore arbitrary. Others should not have the right to make rules for you. Let's just all be good people. Let's treat each other right, and occupy ourselves with doing good things such as saving the whales, fighting climate change, or a thousand other things that we can support with bumper stickers without any need to change our behavior.

Review and Reflect

That is quite an achievement by the father of lies. He has taken the greatest Good News the world has ever known, or could know, and in the minds of multitudes made it bad news! Will you receive or share the genuine Good News of Jesus' sacrificial love and saving plan?

—14—

Entropy

Entropy is the summary term for that aspect of the 2nd Law of Thermodynamics describing the downward flow of energy from order to disorder. There are entire books on the subject. The authorities and all (ALL!) scientific experience state unequivocally, and in agreement, that it applies to the entire physical world without exception. This is the uniform experience at all times, and everywhere.

Everything is spiraling downward from more order to less—everything, with no exceptions. Except . . . EVOLUTION!

The Oxford Dictionary defines *entrophy* as:

1. Noun (mass noun); Physics a thermodynamic quantity representing the unavailability of a system's thermal energy for conversion into mechanical work, often interpreted as the degree of disorder or randomness in the system: the second law of thermodynamics says that entropy always increases with time [count noun] the sum of the entropies of all the bodies taking part in the process.

2. lack of order or predictability; gradual decline into disorder: a marketplace where entropy reigns supreme.

3. (in information theory) a logarithmic measure of the rate of transfer of information in a particular message or language.

Evolutionary scientists never mention this, at least not for public consumption. Even though the textbooks and the experience of all the investigators in every field bear out the conclusion that entropy affects everything, with no exceptions. They, without any evidence of shame on their part, proclaim evolution is the answer, while overriding this law and allowing for the universe to move from disorder to order. Never, of course, acknowledging that this is against all the evidence that science has gathered regarding entropy.

And therefore, it is against common sense and experience. Ah, but when your quest to escape God is frantic enough and desperate enough, you will believe anything no matter how great the evidence is against it. (Spiritual blindness is also a part of it.)

The *theory* of evolution postulates that, starting from nothing, literally chaos, EVERYTHING IS SPIRALING NOT DOWNWARD, BUT UPWARD! Contrary to what you would expect. It is not at all in line with common sense or with experience.

Think of it! Most scientists are insisting that despite all evidence to the contrary, they have found something, not just something, but the very process that tries to explain everything, I mean EVERYTHING...in their flight from God!

Do they have any evidence for their contention that nothing exists beyond the physical? No. But "we're scientists." "You can trust us. Look at our white lab coats! We have given you modern technology! You owe us! How about some respect! Distrust means disrespect. And we've earned it!" Besides in your (unrepentant) hearts, you know it is good news!

We've already seen that evolution offers no explanation of the origins of the laws of physics, in an earlier chapter. Modern technology depends on God's laws of physics, the very One who evolutionists are trying to escape. (Evolutionists use the boundaries made possible by God's laws, to resist Him, and mislead hundreds of millions of people! Shame!)

Review and Reflect

As we have seen, evolution is believed for a wide variety of reasons. I suspect for most people it is the default position... something they haven't given much thought. The scientists believe it; the world accepts it, and, they think "I don't see how it affects me that much."

When you consider that by far the most consequential decision anyone will ever make involves whether or not God exists, and sent His Son to save us both for now and eternity. If the potential consequences were small, you might not put much thought into the decision. But the "God question" entails who you are... a cosmic accident, or made by your Creator in His image.

It involves whether your significance is monumental or trivial. It involves whether you have much meaning, significance, purpose value and dignity, or if you are just a cosmic accident with very little in the way of value, dignity, significance and so on. And, of course, where we will spend eternity is part of the equation!

And when trouble comes, when pain and suffering comes,

when your need is great – is there any hope? In what? In Whom?
The world is too distracted to even consider it.

You can help.

Testing Truth Claims
Correspondence and Coherence

What is true? Who do you trust? Who can you trust? The joke runs "don't trust anyone but your Mother, and even with her you cut the cards!"

The most consequential question you will ever face is regarding God.

There are highly credentialed and powerful people whose life mission is to persuade you that God is a pre-scientific concept... that all religions have their origin in antiquity. These people say that there is no significant difference between faith and superstition, fables, fairy tales and all other pie-in-the-sky, bye-and-bye stories. We are told that they (including God) are all myths.

We need to put all claims to the test of Correspondence. Someone tells us that the check is in the mail. A few days later, we check our mailbox and find that check; it is verified. The claim "corresponds to the reality."

"There is a blue truck in the parking lot" is a truth claim. We can test the claim by sending someone out to check. We send someone. They come back with the report that there is a blue truck in the parking lot. It meets the correspondence test. The claim matches the reality. When many witnesses corroborate the claim, it meets the additional test of coherence.

Can we make this work on the God question? You tell me. I think the world is as would be expected if its origin was created by a Mind. The qualities of:

Order Corresponds with God.
It does not correspond with an explosion.
Organization Corresponds with God.
It does not correspond with an explosion.
Diversity Corresponds with God.
It does not correspond with an explosion.
Complexity Corresponds with God.
It does not correspond with an explosion.
Productivity Corresponds with God.
It does not correspond with an explosion.
Fruitfulness Corresponds with God.
It does not correspond with an explosion.
Intelligibility Corresponds with God.
It does not correspond with an explosion.
Predictability Corresponds with God.
It does not correspond with an explosion.

Each aspect, singly and as a whole, powerfully points to origin by a Mind that is both rational and intentional, collectively and individually.

Evolution's claim of the origin being an explosion in space that was not guided by intentionality, purpose or meaning, does not even begin to correspond with the multitudes of complex processes that are present. From explosions we experience chaos, not order. We experience nonfunctioning disarray, not understandable, intelligible functionality. And so on.

A world that comes into being without any intentionality would look like what? It's hard to say. The above description of the world shouts intention, purpose, meaning, value, and not the cockamamie, unproven *theory* that dismisses and disrespects the Master Architect of the universe, while simultaneously eroding our trust in Him and His Word!

Why would we expect a world without intentionality to have the characteristics of purpose or beneficial outcomes? All the world's features point to God. It CORRESPONDS to what one would expect when God is the source.

Atheists want to dismiss God, yet still enjoy all the beauty and functionality of God's creation. A major reason the scientists promoting evolution are believed and trusted *is modern technology*. The public equates science and evolution. The truth is the declarations of evolution – blind, mindless and without purpose - run counter to the requirements for modern technology.

No intentionality means no purpose. This lie of no purpose is demolished by the twin sciences of ecology and environmentalism, which will be discussed later.

Review and Reflect

Can you explain "correspondence? Coherence?

CHAPTER

---16---

Absurd Things

The *theory* of evolution is no more than an attempt to explain everything, including origins, without any reference to God. In their flight from God, evolutionists have imagined (but never seen) a process they call *natural selection,* that has supposedly phenomenally produced everything we see and experience. Evolutionists realize the god-like qualities of *natural selection*, to be able to accomplish all we see and experience, is likely to provoke the response "Natural Selection" is just your name for God! In anticipation, their own definition of Natural Selection" from Richard Dawkins is described as:

Natural Selection is "Blind, Mindless and without Purpose."

There. That takes care of it, doesn't it? Yeah, maybe, but with no God it requires the belief that:

Nothing Created Everything? Absurd!

Chaos Created Order? Absurd!

Non-Life Created Life? Absurd!

Non-Consciousness Created Consciousness? Absurd!

Non-Personal Created Personal? Absurd!

Non-Rational Created Rational? Absurd!

Blind Created Vision? Absurd!

Deaf Created Hearing? Absurd!

Non-Smelling Created Smelling? Absurd!

Non-Tasting Created Tasting? Absurd!

Non-Tactile Created the Sense of Touch? Absurd!

Non-Caring Created the Nurturing? Absurd!

Not only absurd, but irrational!

Against all common sense and experience!

And, I suppose the list could be added to –

Non-Intuition created Intuition?

Non-Innovating created Innovating?

Non-Justice created Justice?

Non-Loving created Loving?

Non-Problem Solving created Problem Solving?

The list could go on.

Think of it! What are the odds? We are tempted to think – They Can't Be Serious!

And yet they are deadly serious about brainwashing and mind-controlling, convincing the children that evolution is science, that "religion" is superstition, and that God is a pre-scientific concept. Evolutionists also want us to believe that "all scientists affirm that evolution is true! A whole host of other things, upon further examination, prove to not be true as well!

Even if you stopped at the very first one, it would tax the imagination to conceive how desperate the flight from God must be! The evolutionists chide and disparage us for our faith. Looking at that list, I don't know how anyone can have enough faith to know all that, and still be an atheist or agnostic. Yet they are the ones who have accused us of parking our brain at the door!

Evolution's starting point—their Ten Commandments

1) The natural and physical are all that exists.
2) Science is the final arbiter on everything.
3) Faith and superstition are about the same thing.
4) God is a pre-scientific concept.
5) All scientists agree on the validity of evolution.
6) Only our science is allowed in the classroom.
7) We, and only we, decide what is and what is not science.
8) Any science we don't like will be dismissed as "religion."
9) Government, culture and the public will believe just as they are taught.
10) Our pronouncements are final and our rule is absolute.

However, just as a reminder, we must live in the real world—God's World. That means, life with no God is best described as:

Bleak

Despairing

Meaningless

Unfair

Unrelenting

Exhausting

Hopeless

Pain filled
Pointless
We are alone, alienated from God.
We are sometimes the victim, sometimes exploiting others.

Then someone comes along with good news.
There is great joy in finding a purpose greater than oneself.
Joy, meaning, value, purpose, and hope.
We are all guilty before God, but Jesus has paid the price for us
to take away the penalty.
God offers grace to us. Then our gratitude to God fulfills us and
gives us joy.

A lot of people don't like the idea of God. Some of them grow up to be scientists and educators. They began as rebels and yet succeed in convincing multitudes that they are fair, objective, neutral, and trustworthy. Someone must tell the children. We find no reason to think they would be neutral or objective or even fair when (they think) their most cherished *freedoms* are at stake.

Review and Reflect

Which of the above insights are the most real to you? Can you help others realize what they sign on for when God is left out?

——17——

Millions of Fossils; No Transitional Forms

Evolutionists want you to believe that the fossil record is proof of the validity of evolution.

There are millions of fossils in the museums and universities around the world that purport to prove evolution is both valid and scientific: this is held forth as a proof of the *theory* of evolution. A great deal of scholarship and earned credentials testify that this is the case and this is where the discussion is to end. You are to accept without question that it is as the experts say, that evolution provides all the answers, and that all the real scientists are evolutionists and you should just shut up with all your God talk. Is this really the case? Do the fossil collections anywhere exhibit a fossil that is transitional in nature; a fossil that is part bird and part fish, or any other combination of transition from one species to another? Rest assured we would have all seen the pictures if they had any! Not even one. If that is the fact, then they have not made their case that evolution has successfully replaced God and is indeed the answer we must all put our trust in!

The decision to be made about whether or not to believe in God and His Son is by far the most consequential one that anyone will ever make. With God out of the picture we do not have much in the way of dignity, value, significance, meaning or purpose. Yeah we have some dignity, value, significance, meaning or purpose, lasting perhaps seven or eight decades. And then we are gone, and a hundred years from now, with God out of the picture, it won't matter that you ever existed.

And what about now, right now when trouble comes? With God out of the picture, you must face it. No help now, and no help later! And when God's reality is proven, and you are yet rebellious, you face eternity alone. No God means, in the final analysis, no hope. And when someone stronger is tempted to take advantage of you, or even worse, someone you love, if they believe there is no one keeping score, they may find scant reason to resist the temptation.

It is not a good thing that many in society who do not believe in God and His standards, find little reason to resist the opportunity to take advantage of you, or someone you love! Someone pays. You pay. If evolution is the reality, the first law for everyone is survival of the fittest. And we must live by the law of the jungle. That's your habitat when evolution is believed.

And yet they insist that the fossils prove evolution. The absence of transitional forms reveals that it is a lie. They know that. They don't care. Pray for them. And tell the kids!

Review and Reflect

Can you help others see that it is no small thing to leave God out?

Thousands of Books

The existence of thousands of books in the universities and libraries are claimed as proof for evolution. However, the authors begin with the assumption that nothing exists beyond the natural physical world. They don't know that. There is no conceivable way to prove it, so they ignore that fact and write their books with the assumption, but no proof of what they teach.

Evolutionists want you to believe that the thousands of books written by them "prove" that evolution is valid. The universities and research labs across the world have many volumes covering the various aspects of evolution. All written by experts who know more than you! We should say they are written by so-called "experts," with daunting and impressive credentials that are supposed to certify that they know what they are talking about. They uniformly and in lock step declare that the *theory* of evolution is no longer just a *theory*, but has, by virtue of near unanimous support across the scientific community, become, and is now, settled science!

They claim that "micro" evolution "proves" macro evolution. Micro evolution is minor adaptations within a species that are a response to local conditions. This happens over relatively short periods of time, and is observable. They want you to believe these minor adaptations within a species validate "macro" species to species evolution that occurs over millions of years. Again, they have no proof among the millions of fossils. It is a faith position.

So what are we to do in the face of that? This is a main part of the reason that evolution sits astride the globe, ruling and dominating in education, government, law, culture, and in the media, both news and entertainment. And dare we raise our hand and object? Who in the face of such scholarship would dare to object?! And it is intimidating to raise our hand to even ask a question. To question is seen by them as a challenge, a threat. And they can't allow that! Who knows where or to what it might lead?

Evolutionists make all kinds of claims that they offer no proof for. They say things like "Science is Evolution and Evolution is Science." And "all reputable scientists are evolutionists." And "to reject evolution is to make the claim that you are smarter than all the scientists." And "superstition and faith are very much alike." And, "you know, don't you that all religions have their origins in antiquity." And they bamboozle us with a whole lot more. Of course no one person has read all the books claiming that evolution is true. But we can begin to discern the pattern. The books all start with, and assume the validity of evolution and go on from there. Nowhere do they offer justification of why evolution is a better answer than God. (See chapter 1.)

They start on the faulty foundation that nothing created everything! Crazy! That is the fundamental reality of the matter. The real question that begs to be answered is "Tell us why evolution is the better answer?" And they don't venture an opinion. And they don't offer evidence. And they don't have any proof that evolution is valid.

And the reason is they have no objective, independent standard, or protocol or critique by which they can justify the decision to reject God, and assign the source of all life to something else (See chapter 1). So the thousands of books are not a threat to your faith in God when you understand they have no evidence against God. If they had any, you can bet we would all know it!

Review and Reflect

How have they managed to get away with it?

18

They Want to Make Science Replace GOD

Modern science is widely believed to have done away with God; however, there is no conflict between genuine science and God. There is a reason why we have modern technology. It is because the early scientific community was, for the most part, from what was called Christendom, medieval and later Europe. With a Biblical world view where scientists supposed that a reasonable God would create a rational and reasonable world with observable order. And they began to quest to discover that order.

Modern science could have never come out of polytheism, or from a view that the world is an illusion. Faith in God is the reason behind modern science, not from evolution's assumptions. There is a reason why there are laws of physics. Again, if there are laws there has to be a Lawgiver (Chapter 11). Evolution is not science, and has no valid scientific evidence to prove that God IS NOT the author of everything: even the author of evolution. Of course the whole idea of evolution is continual attempt to explain away God and using the guise of science but in fact they are forced to rely on conjecture and speculation.

Evolution deserves no respect.

Destroying confidence in the *theory* of evolution is simple and nontechnical.

You decide if this helps to make the case (*True or False*).

1)   Modern science denies the existence of anything beyond the physical world. *True.* They offer no science as proof. *True.* It is not possible to prove that nothing exists beyond the material world. They and we must accept it on faith. *True.*

The world thinks their rejection of God is a result of their research. The world needs to know that the foundation of evolution is not science as they insist, but their FAITH, having decided beforehand, that God does not exist. They then try to imagine and speculate "how" things came into existence and offer it to an unsuspecting world as SCIENCE! For those who consider God as good news, this should be enough to destroy confidence in the *theory*.

2)   Evolution has not offered the standard by which they justify the rejection of God, but they assign the existence of all matter to something else. *True.*

3)   Evolution has not offered their explanation of the origins of the laws of physics. *True.*

4)   Christians have not examined the character of the originators of evolution. What kind of person would want to find an alternate explanation that leaves out God?

Here are 12 questions you may find helpful, liberating, and easy. A bit of reiteration.

1)   **Are superstition and faith really about the same?**
Sometimes those who find the idea of God inconvenient are tempted to resort to underhanded measures. The similarities of faith and superstition are superficial and the differences are fundamental. Superstition is emotionally based. Faith in God is evidence based. What evidence? Romans 1:20 points to His Creation, the Order, Organization, and Fruitfulness, etc.

When we eat or drink anything, it is an act of faith. We have reason to believe that sanitary protocols have been followed, and we are usually right. When we drive in traffic we are acting in faith. We have a reasonable expectation that others will observe the protocols and most of the time they do. Our faith is evidence based. Faith in God is evidence based, evidence that is self evident, common sense and aligns with our experience.

2)   **Is God really a pre-scientific concept?**
This is evolution's contention and their claim. To suggest because there have always been those who believe in God is to say the idea of God is outdated and therefore unreliable is not honest. But it works. At least with those for whom God is bad news!

3) **Does the world really look like the result of a big explosion in space?**

Not really. We have all seen explosions. They produce disorder, not the exquisite order and orderliness and beauty we all see in nature.

4) **Does Science really claim to be the authority on things that exist beyond the physical and natural world?**

Well, yes. They would have to if their pronouncements against God would carry any weight. They have no evidence against God, but because they are seen as trustworthy they have gotten away with it. So far!

5) **If the *theory* of evolution is true, why does it need the quarantine and censorship of alternate views?**

Good question. Genuine Truth would not need censorship of other views in the schools. And when they encountered opposition, they could, in the great comfort of knowing their position was secure, offer gracious, kind and sympathetic understanding to the unfortunate unenlightened ones. Not what you see. Good athletes enjoy competition, and you would think that if evolutionists really thought they could deliver the goods, they would welcome all competition, knowing that truth would prevail. They don't! They know the pretense would be revealed.

6) **Would not triumphant truth both welcome and relish side by side comparison to vindicate, once and for all the claim of validation?**

Yes. Why not? Yet they don't.

7) **Why is only one view of origins allowed in schools?**

Another good question; Do you suppose they have something to hide? Like not having a standard by which to justify assigning against God? (See chapter 1.)

8) **Why are the thug tactics of stigma, shunning, ostracizing, painful exclusion and negative labeling needed to defend evolution?**

Again, these are telltale signs of lack of evidence. But altogether what you would expect from the kingdom of darkness.

9) **Why is evolution so widely believed; because it is true, or for some other reason?**

Mankind is many things. One perspective is "Body, Soul and Spirit". Another is we have emotions, a mind or intellect, and a will. The resolute will to disbelieve regardless of the evidence indicates the decision for disbelief originated in the Will. When this is the case, the decision to regard God as bad news is not rationally based. And no evidence, no matter how compelling will move them. What else would you expect from those who, from the very inception, set out with determination to find another explanation that leaves out God?

10) **What is the standard used to justify assigning something, to not God, but to something else?**

I don't think they have one. If they did, don't you think we would all know it? Don't you think it would be in every science text, from the lower grades through doctorate levels? Since that is not the case, I think it is safe to declare they don't have one!

It does help explain why they offer no side by side evaluations of competing theories. And it does explain their censorship of competing views. And it does explain their need to resort to thug tactics against all challenges.

11)   **What else is true if the *theory* says we are not made in the image of God but are no more than accidents of nature?**

Without God we have very little meaning, significance value and purpose, and no hope when pain and suffering come. With no God, there is no chance that the suffering might have purpose. No eternity to reap a harvest, remember? Who am I and what should I be doing with my life? You are an image bearer of God. And this makes all the difference in the world! You have the promise "Seek and you shall find." The dogmatic stance of disbelief characterizes the foundation of evolution.

You can choose to doubt evolution honestly.
Before anyone can make an intelligent choice,
the decision must be made: Is God good news or bad news?
What is it going to cost? The cost of believing?
The cost of not believing?

Some like to think that the Garden of Eden was the fairytale
and yet believe that NOTHING created EVERYTHING
and call it science.

Belief that
The unintentional
Created the intentional is ridiculous.

But you are unscientific if you don't go along.
This is self-evident.

It is a form of Child Abuse
To restrict school curriculum to the *theory* of evolution
And to censoring out God.
This is self-evident.

We are questing to do something about it!

Confrontation with evolution.
It is not a legitimate science, as it is perceived by the world.
Our goal is revealing it as the fraud that it is!
A fraud from the inception, where disbelievers,
the enemies of God,
have sought an alternate explanation to replace God.
Most Christian response to the *theory* of evolution
treats it with respect.
Instead it needs to be exposed for the fraud it is.

Fourteen KEYS of Concern

1.   Evolution is a campaign of indoctrination. Picture in your mind's eye tens of millions of children are being marched off to schools that are little more than brainwashing and indoctrination centers, where only one view of origins is allowed. The churches know this. The pastors and denominations know this. And yet it continues. Why? It is because until now we haven't had the simple and non-

complex and self-evident answers that are easy to understand and pass along.

2. Why we are convinced evolution is true?
   a.) Because it is what we were taught by those we trusted. And because it is what our teachers were taught by those they trusted. And so on up the line. We all, everyone not engaged in basic research, have no hands-on experience. We all take it on faith believing evolution is trustworthy, reliable, and having no agenda they champion!
   b.) Many are easily persuaded because "No God" is perceived as "good news."
   c.) We don't know what or how much, we don't know. And may be tempted to think "if I knew what my professors know, maybe I would not believe in God either". This is profoundly not the case, as we are in the process of proving.

3. There are two ways to look at the *theory* of evolution; first, to see it as a colossal fortress sitting astride the world and ruling in the education of our children, as an invincible stronghold, defeating all foes. Secondly, their aim is dominance in science, education, government, the judiciary, the media both news and entertainment and through the culture in general. And this is the general perception. However, we can now view it as only and no more than an alternate explanation of things that makes no room for God.

4. Their tactics are the major giveaway of the bankruptcy of their lack of genuine science. If they really believe that

evolution is "Settled Science, as claimed, there would be no need to resort to censorship. And no need for Mafia and bullying tactics. No need to list the tragic history of the atrocities of religion and then to equate religion to God and dismiss them together, as if religion and God were one and the same. No need for dissimulation that "you know, don't you that all religions have their origins in antiquity?" And no need for intimidation that keeps school faculty, as well as students, toeing the line. There is abundant evidence of numerous faculty denials of tenure for questioning the validity of the *theory*. You are required to confess "Evolution is science and science is evolution." Anything else and you are labeled a heretic, an outcast, and an enemy to be dealt with. This reaches all the way to you and me. Say anything that challenges the evolutionists and you will be stigmatized as ignorant, poorly educated and against science.

5. Truth claims: Can we know what is true? Correspondence and coherence are tests we use against truth claims. Does whatever is claimed line up with whatever exists? (See chapter 16.)

    For example, we say, "The headline in today's paper says (such and such)." We consult a copy of the paper and verify that it does indeed correspond, and confirm the claim. The test of correspondence is met. Many others check the claim. They all report the same result. The answer coheres, it holds together by the report of many witnesses. The claim both corresponds and coheres. It is true.

6. We don't need a scientist in a white lab coat like the TV series Cosmos - There is a great deal we can know on our own. Look at the world and see a very high degree of Order, not at all what you would expect from a big explosion in space. Not only is there Order and Organization, which corresponds most powerfully with God, but it also comes with great Fruitfulness and Productive output, which most powerfully corresponds with God, not at all what we would expect from an explosion. Add to the Order, Organization, Fruitfulness and Productivity, a very great Diversity of things, but also an astonishing and mind boggling Complexity, which most powerfully corresponds with God. Again nothing you would expect from an explosion. Everything you would expect from a Mind, and one astonishment after another, is it all, to a great extent Predictable, or Lawful and Dependable! This idea most powerfully corresponds with God, not at all likely to be the outcome of an explosion.

Finally, or maybe not, it is to a very great extent, Understandable! Comprehensible! Intelligible WHICH MOST POWERFULLY CORRESPONDS WITH GOD! Who would have guessed it?

7. DNA and the denial of Intelligent Design -If the proof of the planned, intricate, and amazing design of the elegant DNA helix does not bespeak a Designer to you, you are choosing ignorance. Facts are stubborn things! Can you imagine the degree of resolve (read "faith"?) it takes for a scientist committed to an irrational stake in the God denying and faith destroying *theory* of Evolution, to understand and know the

encyclopedic intelligible information in the DNA of every living thing, and to insist, THINK OF IT! INSIST! That its origin is Blind, Mindless and Without Purpose or Intention? The public thinks Evolutionists are Neutral, Objective, Fair and Trustworthy and as not having an agenda. Who will tell them?

8. Consider the miraculous aspects of today's date (Chapter 22) Kingdoms, empires, nations, states and provinces have, throughout history entered into treaties, alliances and other arrangements for commerce and for peace. Those were mostly local in nature and may have lasted only for short durations. The Roman Republic lasted four or five hundred years before becoming the Roman Empire. The empire lasted about four hundred more. So when we find an arrangement lasting two millennia, and is global in its reach, we can say it is unprecedented and not the result of manmade treaties. Today's date testifies to events in a small backwater province. It points to a miraculous birth, a sinless life of notable events ranging from giving sight to the blind, healing the sick, raising the dead feeding multitudes, and other supernatural events. It points to a mock trial and death by crucifixion, resurrection and ascension into heaven.

It marks Jesus Christ as authentic and as who He claimed to be as well as makes authentic and reliable everything he taught, including Eden!

9. The origins of the *theory* of evolution (Chapter 5) before

Darwin, God was viewed as a perfectly valid explanation of the Origins of everything. But there were some to whom God was seen as an impediment, a spoiler who prohibits the very things we find most appealing. How are we to view the nature and character of men running from God? Would you trust them with your credit card or checkbook or with your vote or with the education of your children? These are those who destroy your children's faith and confidence in the God of the Bible? These are the ones trying to persuade us that you and everyone else are only accidents of nature as society crumbles.

10. With our minds eye, let's look over the shoulder of a basic research scientist (Chapter 1). Darwin has just turned the world upside down. Multitudes of scientists have returned to their labs. Across the disciplines of Biology, Botany, and all the way to Zoology, all the processes and outcomes are being re-examined. Hundreds and thousands of decisions are being made. When this process and these outcomes are fully understood they will be attributed to evolution or to God. Our scientist is about to reach a conclusion. He hesitates, reflects, and finally assigns it to evolution. May we ask how you made the decision? We ask? He reflects, ponders and finally answers. "It just seems like the better answer." He says. But, we ask, "What standard or protocol or criteria did you use to justify the decision?" They have not disclosed the standard used to justify assigning to evolution and not to God. They don't have one. They haven't needed one. Speculation, conjecture and wishful

thinking and the allure of "freedom" have been enough. Think about it. If they had a justifying standard you would expect it to be prominent in science classes on every level, in every textbook, and on every exam. This explains why there is never a side by side comparison. Not with Creation Science. Not with Intelligent Design. Not with Specified Complexity or Irreducible Complexity. Now we can understand their being forced to resort to thug tactics against all challenges. They can't have a side by side comparison because they have no standard by which to justify assigning to one, evolution, and not to God! Is this not self-evident? How long will they get away with it?

11. The loss of Meaning - When we no longer see ourselves as image-bearers of God and we are told we are unplanned and unintended accidents of nature, then not much meaning, dignity, significance, value and purpose are left. When shooters kill, isn't it likely they have bought into a "low" view of what it means to be human? The ensuing outcry against guns always follows.

Why does the cry never come to allow God back in the schools? Because we haven't known that evolution is not science, as claimed. But it is all a colossal fake. At one time or another, we have wondered about the meaning of life. The *theory* of evolution validates that feeling of meaninglessness.

Here's how to put that lie to rest; if humans have no meaning, then neither does anything else. It is all futile and without hope. However, the scientific disciplines of Ecology and Environmentalism attest to the significance of all things.

If everything else has purpose, so do you! You have meaning and value and science proves it.

12. The Origins of the Laws of Nature and of Physics are nowhere explained by evolution - I suppose the reason why is that they point to a Lawgiver! The very one they are trying to do away with. They cannot spin a convincing "origin" so they remain quiet and hope we don't notice.

13. Entropy (Chapter 15) is a summary term for that part of the 2nd law of thermodynamics that says everything is moving from a more ordered state to a less ordered state - The authorities emphasize "all," and insist "everything!" The *theory* of evolution claims the opposite.

    Evolution requires that everything is in the process of becoming more organized and complex; spiraling upward. Not downward as all the experience of legitimate science testifies. This contradicts the 2nd law of thermodynamics.

14. Evolution's only reason for existing is to attempt to provide a plausible explanation of how things came to be - without God - It has no other purpose. They might claim it to be a more up to date way of approaching the data, but that won't wash. It insists on leaving God out and this decision is made before they even enter the lab! Leaving God out and providing an alternate explanation is the only reason evolution exists, indeed, the only "need" for it.

By ignoring God you face eternity alone and without hope, with uncertainty at every turn, with little meaning, value, significance or purpose. Examine yourself. Why do you think God is good news or bad news? Yes, bad things do happen, but if there is no God in the picture, then everything is a mere accident and without intention. You can say "I don't like it yet we need an unmoving standard (God) of right and wrong, good and bad, to be able to make the determination that it is bad. And, with God out of our picture bad things still happen. But with no God they must be seen as meaningless. Think of it! All the pain and suffering in the world, over the ages would fill all the oceans and with no God it is meaningless and hopeless!

With a God who is holy, righteous and loving – we have the possibility of struggling to trust God with what we don't understand and what we must endure! No God? No meaning and no hope. Without God we are just expressing our opinions when we declare anything "wrong."

Without an unmoving standard of right and wrong, of good or bad, everything is just your preference or your opinion. You don't approve of pain and suffering? OK, but without a standard to differentiate, it's just "your opinion!"A life apart from God is like being set adrift without direction without purpose and without hope. All that is left is a life of meaningless despair and hopelessness. No wonder more and more people are giving in to the impulse to take their own lives.

The whole world is filled with purposefulness and intentionality. Evolution emphatically and vociferously denies that God is the reason for that! Do they offer any evidence or proof that God does not exist? Of course not! They haven't needed to.

They have successfully made their case to a gullible and (mostly) unbelieving world, eager to get along without Him. However, a closer look reveals that it is self evident and common sense and lines up with experience that God exists! He is the answer and not a big explosion in space. And that is really Good News!

Review and Reflect

Which insight resonates best with you? Can you tell others?

CHAPTER

19

Fine-Tuning and Multi-Verses

Scientists have discovered a significant number of instances of exquisite fine-tuning which points away from a big explosion in space and points powerfully towards the Creator God of Scripture. Some are too technical in nature for the untrained mind, of which, I am one. So, for our purposes we consider things easy to visualize. For example: The Goldilocks effect.

If the sun or moon were 10% larger or smaller, or 10% nearer or farther, if Earth's rotation were 10% faster or slower, or it's tilt on its axis were 10% greater or smaller, life as we know it would not exist on Earth. The ecological balance of the Earth seems finely-tuned and precariously balanced. Do you feel all this is more likely to be the result of a blind, mindless and without purpose process or of a Creator? (See "Take the quiz" at https://www.servetheking.org/bible-basic-quick-notes.)

These are a handful of examples of fine tuning.

There are at least a couple of dozen other examples verified by scientists that the effects are precisely what is needed to sustain life.

These arguments for God were gaining traction and were the kinds of science easily grasped by the "untrained" general public and was causing enough challenge to the theory of evolution that it was decided that something should be done about it. And something was done.

From out of nowhere we are "spoon fed," . . .

"There is no reason" we were magisterially told, "that there could not be an infinite number of universes!" And, this being the case, it would be a lead pipe cinch that in an infinite number of universes, there would have to be one with all the fine-tuning necessary to sustain life as we know it!" And, as luck would have it, it's ours! Our universe is the one out of an infinite number of possible universes is the one fine-tuned for life. Aren't we lucky! And still no need for a spoil sport God.

It seems to me that is exactly what has happened, at least in the evolution camp. The problem is the church and the world, having been defeated so many times in their presentation of Creation Science, Intelligent Design science, Specified Complexity and Irreducible Complexity. They have, so to speak, had their heads handed back to them on a platter for the most part and remained quiet. And it seems no one has stepped up and said what needs to be said:

> "Just because evolutionists find no reason not to imagine an 'infinite number' of universes, there is also no reason to need an infinite number of universes—except to escape from God!"

118

There is the rebuttal. There is no reason to believe in a multi-verse. No basis in scientific discovery. No need of one except to escape. How much wiser to believe in an infinite all wise, Creator God! The goal of this work is to provide an easy to understand basis for a bold and confident witness and life of faith for the Christian and the world.

— 20 —

Ecology and the Meaning of Life

Ecology and Environmentalism are tasked with the study of relationships of the various aspects of nature.

The Oxford English Dictionary defines *ecology* as the branch of biology that deals with the relations of organisms to one another and to their physical surroundings.

It is being reported that we have neglected our responsibilities and are wreaking havoc across the globe. And that the situation is perilous and remedies must be immediate and forthcoming or our very survival is in doubt. There appears to be some disagreement among the experts, but we are in their debt for their labors. Who would have guessed the lives of the literally millions of species were so entwined and inter-dependent?

Science News: How many species on Earth? About 8.7 million

Date: August 24, 2011

Source: Census of Marine Life

Summary: *About 8.7 million (give or take 1.3 million) is the new, estimated total number of species on Earth -- the most precise calculation ever offered -- with 6.5 million species on land and 2.2 million in oceans. Announced by the Census of Marine Life, the figure is based on a new analytical technique.*

Don't you find it remarkable that all of these life forms are born into a habitat where they can thrive? While some species are similar and thrive in swampy or desert environments, others in very hot and dry and some in very cold and wet, and everything in between, they find a place to live where they can thrive and survive; this points to purpose! And purpose points to God.

There are only two explanations of why this is. One explains how a Creator God made both the creatures AND their habitats. The other is that "Natural Selection" described by its promoters as "Blind, Mindless and without Purpose or Intention" created both the creatures and their "made to order" habitats. No rational or logical evidence would lead us to believe that. Unless one found the idea of God Bad News! You and I must consciously lead our lives as witness to the goodness of God.

The order, organization, diversity, complexity, fruitful and productive outcomes, and predictability and dependability, and the intelligibility and interpretability of the data, both separately and collectively powerfully correspond with God, and no way nor to any degree correspond to a blind, mindless, and purposeless source.

If the testimony of ecology is accepted, then everything has meaning and purpose. The reign of evolution has caused many to believe their lives are without meaning and purpose. If everything else has value, significance, meaning, and purpose – then so do you! God exists. He loves you! And you are separated from Him and under a curse by your sins. But you don't have to remain that way.

He has paid the penalty for your sins, and He will make you as new in relationship to Him. He has overcome death, and you can have a new beginning.

Review and Reflect

What are the odds?

—— 21 ——

Miraculous Aspects of the Calendar

What is the greatest, the most stupendous, the most gigantic, the most towering and monumental thing that ever happened to you? When I asked a friend, after a moment he said "I don't think it has happened yet!" What is the greatest event you have heard about, or read about, or were taught? For Christians it would be Jesus Christ's resurrection from the dead. The unbelievers do not think that. However, the existence of our global calendar is a monumental testament to the empty tomb.

Oh I know that the resolve of the disbelievers can, by tortuous reasoning, seem to "explain" it away.

But the most straightforward answer points to an empty tomb.

- The fact that virtually all the world uses the same calendar is a monumental fact, and not a small one. The astronomical origins of days, months and years. We get the term "day" from the 24 hours it takes for

1 rotation of the earth.

- The Lunar month is 28 days. The same duration as a woman's menstrual cycle. 13 months of 28 days equals 364 days or one year. Of course we now know that the Solar year is 365.25 days for each revolution of Earth around the Sun. The fraction requires a "leap" year every 4 years where February is given a "leap" day, February 29.
- Unless the leap year is divisible by 100.
- And not divisible by 400.
- Globally all modern cultures conform to these standards.
- A "week "has no astronomical component, yet it is everywhere observed.
- Where did "week" originate? It has no astronomical foundation.
- Believe it or not - The Book of Genesis. And it is observed globally.

When transactions occur between cultures like Muslim, North Korean and Chinese, that have their own starting points, the Western calendar is used as a point of common agreement. The most likely explanation of the global reach of the calendar and its two thousand years' time span is that it is God-ordained. It finds its origin, its starting point from Jesus. It takes a monumental occurrence to produce a monumental result. It is a monumental outcome that the calendar spans the globe.

In cause and effect, the outcome tends to be proportional to the cause: The greater the outcome, (global) the greater the cause (God).

If Jesus Christ rose from the dead that would be the greatest event of history! If He rose from the dead, that authenticates what He said. He said "I am The Way, The Truth, and The Life. No one comes to the Father except by Me" (John 14:6).

Around the world we speak numerous languages and dialects (and use the same calendar). We drive on different sides of the road (and use the same calendar). We measure in metric, or in feet, inches and miles (and use the same calendar). We use different electrical plugs and outlets (and use the same calendar). And we read from left to right while others, from right to left (and use the same calendar). And there are many other differences from culture to culture. In some cases the differences in what we like to eat is off the charts! And in spite of all the disagreements and preferences, we use the same calendar. Wonder why?

This global use of a calendar agreeing on the same starting date is unprecedented in human history. We have records of treaties and trade agreements and records of accord between nations, kingdoms, empires and countries throughout history.

They were mostly local in nature and short term, lasting only for the duration of the reigning monarch. The rise of a new ruler ended the arrangement and brought forth a new one by either negotiation, or politics, or by war. Some things never change.

So what are we to make of an agreement among nations that is global in its reach, and has endured for more than two thousand years? It is clear on the face of it that the answer is not merely a political one.

Rather it points back in time to a "never before and never after series of events that divide history." Events that the now documented (70 A.D. Chapter 7) eyewitness accounts testify to have occurred in a small backwater province of the late Roman Empire. Events as diverse as a virgin birth, a sinless life filled with miracles of healing the sick, raising the dead, feeding the 5,000, walking on water, and the execution of a man found innocent by a Roman court, and guilty by a Hebrew court, who rose from the dead, was seen by the disciples and ascended into Heaven before more than five hundred witnesses. Now that is enough to explain the global reach for 2000 years of your calendar!

The calendar proves with unmatched majesty and certainty that what Jesus taught is true. What more clarity could we ask? What other explanation is plausible? Finding no other rational explanation, the enemy tries to deemphasize the impact by a campaign to change the common usage from A.D. (Anno Domini – The year of our Lord) to C.E. Common Era and B.C.E. before Common Era. It's too early to say if they will get away with it. Resist! Add AD to every date you write. Now you have something to say about it! Please start adding to every check you write and every document you sign the A.D. testimony that it is Anno Domini – The Year of our Lord. And ask family and friends to, as well. It can open the door to a witnessing opportunity.

That today's date is agreed on by the governments around the world is an example of what is called, in philosophical discussion, a brute fact. Remember, one aspect of the law of causality, usually described as cause and effect, is that outcomes or effects tend to be proportional to their causes. A firecracker produces a firecracker size effect. A hand grenade, a blockbuster bomb, and a thermonuclear device, tend to produce effects proportional to their size, strength and power.

Review and Reflect

Now you know and have a reason to believe. Today the global church numbers more than two and a half billion people who identify as Christian. Can there be any doubt that today and every day that the name of Jesus will be spoken tens of millions of times around the globe daily mostly in praise, but, alas, often in cursing.

Alas, the world knows and experiences this! The attempt to explain the calendar apart from God is, at best tenuous and tentative. The calendar is global by divine decree. Common sense – unless you are fleeing God. If you have not already done so, I hope by now that you are at least willing to consider that God is good news.

CHAPTER
—— 22 ——

Evolution's Bitter Harvest

The schools are looking more and more like prisons. They have security fencing with controlled access along with metal detectors and uniformed security guards. What happened? How has it come to this? Sociologists might point to a number of factors, but none are more significant than the natural outcomes of the exclusive teaching of the *theory* of evolution.

The theory of evolution led to the dictates of the Supreme Court banning the display of the Ten Commandments in schools and other public buildings. And why not! "Science" had succeeded in banishing God from the minds of the people and the public square. And, if no "God" then no Eden and no "fall!" Mankind has not fallen as the primitives believed, but was on the ascendant. And, with the help of science and modern technology, ascend to the paradise so longed for. Who needs God? We can do it ourselves! That is the political vision to this day.

When we are convinced that we have descended (ascended?) from apes, or other animals, why should we be surprised when some of us begin to act that way! When you are convinced that there is no God, that there is no originator of rules and laws beyond other mere humans, why the surprise when some challenge your right to make rules for others?

If you are what has come to be called an "alpha male" and you are powerful and skilled at forcing your will upon others, why not? Isn't that the norm in the animal kingdom, from whence we supposedly all emerged? And who gets to decide what's right and wrong when all laws are from mere men, who are just like you and our legislators, who are likewise indoctrinated, scoff at the ancient wisdom and make up the rules as they go along.

Some have tried to justify homosexuality on the grounds that it is observed among animals. Cannibalism is also observed in nature. Point made.

Dr. Spock scorned the ancient wisdom of *"Folly is bound up in the heart of a child, but the rod of discipline will drive it from him."* (Proverbs 22:15, ESV) He equates physical punishment with "hitting the child" and with bullying. So the children enter first grade, many of them from broken homes, and they have never been subdued in their entire lives. Teachers must abide by regulations thought up by others, and are not allowed to meet the child's needs, that is, of correction and molding and shaping them into productive members of society, and the child endures 12 years of forced attendance – and never once is quelled or subdued.

Entering, or trying to enter the workforce, they are mystified! The style and conduct and behavior that served them well, so far, is not acceptable in the workplace. The market is ruthless and entrepreneurs must do their very best to compete, and a well-trained and responsive staff is a de rigueur requirement.

Criminal justice suffers from leaving God out of the picture. Incarceration is very expensive and it is "cruel." The ancient wisdom provides for humane corporal punishment but this has been eliminated as inhumane. You could make the case that imprisonment and solitary confinement is also inhumane, and expensive...and the recidivism rate shows, not very effective. Proverbs 22:15 says,

Foolishness is bound in the heart of a child but the rod of correction will drive it far from him.

God's way is better, but we need to feel good about ourselves.

Early on, sometime before high school, we were likely told that evolution was the scientific explanation for how things are, and that God was the religious explanation. And it went downhill from there. We are led from "science is modern and tangible," to "God is a pre-scientific concept that no one has seen for a while." Beliefs have consequences. I either saw or heard about a photograph of a bear eating the carcass of a deer and a skunk was eating with him. Now the bear will not share his dinner with any other and is powerful enough to enforce that against all others. Except the skunk! Why? The cost is too great.

The courage to speak against evolution can be very costly. They have made it so.

It is man-made rules that contend against scriptural corporal punishment, administered with restraint and mercy that require chain link fences and uniformed guards and metal detectors at schools. Sufficient and appropriate on the spot discipline were adequate in the past. Have you seen on the news several policemen

133

required to take into custody one person? It is because they operate under rules that they must not inflict any discomfort on anyone taken into custody.

Why does it take a squad of police to arrest one suspect? Why the chain link fence at school? It is because the cost of disobedience is not great enough. Raise the costs of disobedience and lower the costs to taxpayers of compliance.

Apply the "board of education to the seat of learning."

Biblical standards work better than evolution's answers.

Review and Reflect

Do you see how not having an unmoving standard of right and wrong, that is God, as revealed through His Word; you are headed down uncharted paths that lead to where you won't want to go?

Evolution's Impact on Society

God's Creation View	Evolutionary View
God	No God
Divine Creation	Evolution
Supernatural Man	Natural Man
Christ Centered Life	Self Centered Life
Biblical Guidelines	Values Clarification
Absolute Standards	Situation Ethics
Obey God's Commands	No God - Obey Self
Moral Accountability	Self-indulgent Behavior
Human Value & Purpose	Survival of the Fittest
Long Term Gratification	Immediate Gratification
Internal Self Government	External Government
Sacrificial Living	Self-indulgent Living
Serve Others	Serve Self
Hope - Faith	No Hope
Eternal Life	Death

23

The World Sees God as Adversary

It seems to a lot of people that God—at least the God of Scripture—is bad news? Wonder why? Mankind has a pretty good thing. God is the source of our dignity, meaning, value, significance, purpose, and when troubles come, as they always do, hope that there is:

Someone to run to.

Someone to find shelter in.

Someone to provide all our needs.

Many believe mankind is not free and they seek and demand that freedom; it seems a good and righteous thing. But, wasn't mankind basically free? Couldn't they do most anything they wanted, except to eat of the tree of good and evil?

Well, yes.

But the tree was there, and it seemed arbitrary to be denied access to it. And the enemy's suggestion was that something good, desirable and beneficial was arbitrarily and unnecessarily being withheld. And man bought it. And we are buying it still. You and

I today are in somewhat the same position. We have appetites, inclinations, drives, and desires that demand to be fulfilled; to be satisfied. The temptation can be overwhelming and God gets in the way.

Why shouldn't we be free to follow our inclinations to "scratch where it itches," to go with the flow? After all it is our nature, isn't it? And we find no reason to deny ourselves – except God. So it can be tempting to view God as a kind of cosmic spoil sport. A cranky old man who is concerned that someone somewhere is enjoying themselves, and having a good time! So when we are faced with blandishments suggesting that God is out-of-date, and belonging to a pre-scientific era, and no longer necessary to explain the forces of nature, why not then join the millions that look to science with gratitude and thanksgiving for having delivered us from such an old grouch!

When this vaunted freedom is announced by scholars with credentials from institutions of "higher learning," (they often have a lower view) they often have little or no faith in God. Many of them worship at the altar of science and find no need for a God. That science indeed has in a sense, replaced God. It is unquestioningly received as liberating good news.

Don't be surprised if your children are told by some professor in biology or other science class, something like this. "You are here to learn and what you learn will likely be beyond the education of your parents. So, don't be concerned if they don't understand or agree with modern science. You will be wise to not take them on in discussion, because, not having access to what you are learning, they will likely not be open to it and only grief will follow."

Do the children find this news welcome and liberating? Some do. And it doesn't help if puberty and hormones are entering the picture about the same time. So, parents, at some point down the road are not prepared to push these topics aside. And they, without confrontation attend church with you less and less and begin to live as their companions, in lifestyles that are not wise. You are less able to engage them in spiritual things. You and God have become adversaries for them. You are obstacles to the life that is luring them further and further away from God. What can we do? For starters, let's step back a bit and try to understand some of the *whys* of God's laws.

Fundamentally, when God says "NO," He is saying "don't hurt yourself and others!" This may not be readily understood or received. We need to make it *foundational* in our own lives before we can enter the campaign. Yes, a long war and not just a brief battle. This one insight will liberate, but it must be learned.

At five or six-years-old, we were learning so much. Our parents were guiding and equipping us for maturity and a productive and abundant life on our own. At that age we could not know there were reasons why we should not eat as much candy or sweets as we wanted. We could not perceive that there were dangers if we played in the street and other dangers of heights and falling, or sharp instruments and injury, or dozens of other things. So, being five or six, and not having learned by experience ourselves, God gave us parents to set limits. This is now self-evident as a good thing. Left alone with no guidance we would have experienced much more pain than we did, and might not have survived childhood.

So, now as adults, thinking we know it all, or at least enough to run (ruin?) our own lives, we make choices that sometimes prove disastrous. It would not be surprising if God views us as even more clueless about spiritual things as adults, than when we were at five or six about what was wise and safe.

God's laws are the safe path through life.

When our experiences can make it seem like life is a jungle, or swamp or desert, God's laws are the safe path through the swamp, or jungle, or desert. God's rules are His gracious offer for us to learn "the easy way," that is by faith and by obedience rather than failing and learning the hard way. Don't be like those, who on their death bed, realize "I would have been better off if I had listened to God's way." Treating others with respect and dignity and not violating their rights by taking advantage of them, is not only moral and right, but is a principle even recognized and taught in the business schools of the world.

God's moral laws are just as real as the laws of physics. Disregard the law of gravity and the consequences are immediate. If you lie or steal or disregard God's "pattern" about sexual relations being reserved for marriage between one man and one woman, the consequences might take a while, but we will come to understand better that it is in His great providential love that God provides the rules for life.

Review and Reflect

You must believe in God, and must believe His rules are for our benefit in order to see them as loving and beneficial.

PART 2:

THE GOD FACTOR

24

Feeling Good About Myself

*Since they did not know the righteousness of God
and sought to establish their own, they did not submit
to God's righteousness.* —Romans 10:3, NIV

The need to feel good about ourselves, to justify ourselves is a universal trait. It is more obvious in some than in others. Having fled from God and not understanding His righteousness, (and its immense personal benefits) we try to establish our own.

So we decide we will not murder, or rob banks. We will treat others well when we are having a good day. We will do all sorts of nice things to feel good about ourselves...maybe even put a "save the whales" sticker on our car. We will keep score and feel very good about our record. "You don't need to believe in God to be a good person!"

And when temptation comes in whatever form, we tell ourselves it's really not hurting anyone and besides no one ever will know, and we think our escape from God is complete. When you see others, in their desperate attempt to *measure up*, and resort to *virtue signaling,* we must avoid the impulse to call their hand. That would be cruel beyond words. Self-respect can vary from individual to individual, but the need to feel good about ourselves, to measure up is universal.

We learn to develop taboos that by our choice, we resolve to not participate in them and we also reserve the right to decide what we will enjoy. Yet, being human, our nature is to "want what we want," to take charge of our lives...to decide for ourselves who and what we will be. Here's what scripture says about self righteousness: Isaiah 64:6 "...all of our righteousness are as filthy rags...!" God cannot endure sin. If He could, He would never have sacrificed His Son!

So when we are told:

Evolution is a liberating scientific discovery!

You are sovereign!

Pursue whatever you want!

Make all your dreams come true!

And live as you were intended – In charge of your life!

Who is anyone else but me to decide for me!

(Think of the sad song) *My Way!*

And no consequences!

This explains the colossal success of the *theory* of evolution as an alternate explanation that has no room for God and the reason why we are so willing to "park our brains at the door." For believers in God it is not in order to have our own way.

So, in our need to feel good about ourselves, to measure up, we join teams helping the poor, feeding the hungry. You might be surprised how good a *fight climate change* sticker on my car makes me feel and who knows what else, all in the vain attempt to avoid God. By *doing good* we manage to feel good about ourselves without having to change our behavior. Again God's declaration: "But we are all as an unclean thing, and all our righteousness are as filthy rags; and we all do fade as a leaf, and our iniquities, like the wind, have taken us away" (Isaiah 64:6).

God's plan, the Gospel, removes the need for us to struggle to measure up.

Review and Reflect

How does the Enemy succeed in clouding the issue, and how we can help others with this issue?

Really God News! You Are Loved

*The Spirit you received does not make you slaves,
so that you live in fear again; rather, the Spirit you
received brought about your adoption as sonship. And
by Him we cry, 'Abba, Father.'* (Rom. 8:15, NIV)

What is that foreign word doing in my English Bible? When the King James Version was translated in 1611, and they came to the word Abba (Hebrew/Aramaic origin and even used today in Israel), they knew that the literal translation was *Daddy* or *Papa*. They were overwhelmed at the idea of addressing the Author of all creation in such an intimate way.

After much consternation and debate the decision was made to not translate it, but to transliterate it. And it stands today as Abba, Father. You and I should take courage that our God looks on us in the most intimate of terms. He is our Papa, our Daddy. Rejoice and triumph in it!

God is good news and Jesus is God in the flesh. He is the God of love. Not the wretched caricature of the god of the evolutionist's feverish imagination that must be fled from at any and all costs.

If your decision to disbelieve is rooted in the deep resolve of the will, then it is unlikely that anything you learn in this book will change that. But if you can be open to the possibility that God is *good news*, put your brain in gear, and let's have an adventure!

"Gospel" means good news. The good news is, among other things, that even though God knows every wrong choice you and I have ever made, He loves us still. That is great good news.

God says: That Christ died for you!

God says: You are lost and under His curse, but you don't have to remain there!

God says: That your sins were dealt with by the death of the Savior!

God says: You therefore do not have to deal with His justice and face Him in judgment!

God says: That therefore, He doesn't have anything against you!

God says: He loves you and He has broken down all the barriers between you and Him, and you can come to Him boldly on the grounds of His grace! And there is more. It gets better and better!

Contrast this with what the Devil wants you to believe.

Satan says: God hates you!

Satan says: This whole salvation thing is a trick to rob you of your freedom!

Satan says: Yeah, it can look good, but there's a catch.

"Everything that you like to do is forbidden by God," Satan

says, and there's no proof. It's all pie in the sky bye and bye. The deep resolve of unbelievers shows that they do not know the Good News. Rather, the father of lies, Satan, has convinced them that the very best news that could ever be, is not good news at all, and that it is some kind of trap, a deception, to rob them of their freedom.

In Eden the temptation was "you will be like God, knowing good from evil." That has come to mean enslavement or a loss, a deception so great that men will believe the most absurd, preposterous things in their frantic flight from God. Like what? Like "Nothing created everything" and a whole lot more.

And when evolutionists don't accept God, when the case they are trying to make against God is weak, and they fudge or embellish the *evidence*, they have decided that after death there is only nothingness. (They have no way of knowing this, but believe and promote it anyway!) With no One in charge, why should we be surprised if, having little reason to resist the temptation, they give in, and try to make their case dishonestly?

This would help explain the rage expressed when anyone dares to challenge the reigning view. Jesus said "I am the way, the truth and the life. No man comes to the Father but through Me." (John 14:6, NIV) The truth can afford to be kind and considerate. The lie must defend itself by any means available, not allowing any challenge to avoid being slapped down. It works. You don't see them giving ground anywhere, do you?

God Is the Unmoving Standard

Unless there is an unmoving standard of right and wrong, good and bad, then everything is pretty much up for grabs. That would render all acts subjective, meaning to be decided on individually, and varying from person to person. God is the unmoving standard for right and wrong. This is their reason for trying to get rid of God. Is the evolutionist correct to protest? What is behind God's provision of rules and limits on behavior?

The cosmos is under the authority of God's laws and therefore operates in orderly and predictable ways. This makes science and modern technology possible. On a personal level we can go our own way at our peril. If you abuse alcohol, it may be a while before the consequences begin to reveal themselves. On the other hand, violate the law of gravity from your rooftop and the consequences are immediate.

God's laws and prohibitions are for our safe paths through life, through the jungles, swamps and deserts of life. When God says "don't," He is saying "Trust Me, don't hurt yourself and others!" The laws are an expression of His loving concern for us. The laws are our friends. Trust God, live and thrive!

The disbeliever's focus on *freedom* is such that he doesn't realize that, with God out of the picture, he is no longer a being "made in the Image...", but only an accident of nature. His *freedom* is costing him the loss of God as the foundational basis for his dignity, self-worth, value, significance, and any basis for hope. (What a poor trade, and it is likely he will see others this way as well as without much value.)

When pain and suffering come, as they eventually do, the unbeliever has no meaning, except the pain and suffering, which are very real. There's no hope when God is out of the picture. Those losses are a very considerable price to pay for this vaunted *freedom*, which, at best, can be *enjoyed* for only seven or eight decades. That is definitely not a good trade!

Consider: Evolution's denial of God pretends to be based on authentic science. And it is received as GOOD NEWS by many. It would not be seen as pretense if they could offer even one fact of evidence that weighed against God. They give the impression they have tons of *scientific* evidence. That the *theory* is now "settled science." Yet, they never tell us what the strongest evidence against God is. Only smoke and mirrors… stuff about "billions of years" and "scientists all agree." But the truth is, they don't have any sound evidence. And, on our side, there are many scientists who are people of faith in God…and reject evolution.

Don't you think that if unbelieving scientists had even a single scientific fact proving God does not exist, they would make sure we all knew it?

Review and Reflect

Consider the beautiful and protective applications of God's Ten Commandments. They have protected us and others in so many ways over the centuries! Conversely, these laws have revealed man's capacity for evil, strongly pointing to our need for the Savior. Imagine if everyone lived by New Testament standards, it would almost be heaven on earth.

The Rapid Spread of Christianity

Historians wonder at the rapid spread of early Christianity across the Middle East. Within the first two or three centuries it had "conquered" much of the known world. Not conquered in the same sense of Islam. Islam is documented as a war of conquest and pillage.

Early Christians knew Jesus said "My kingdom is not of this world." Their goal was not territory in the geographic sense, but of living out the teachings of Jesus boldly and with great confidence, and telling the good news that this life was not the whole story. Many times pain and suffering that comes to all was divinely allowed and was used to shape and develop character, and the outcomes would be revealed in another world. Finally, it was our job to love God and people and to trust God in the midst of our present circumstances.

Since everyone is an image-bearer of God, each enjoyed significant value and worth and were not to be exploited or taken advantage of, but were to be accorded respect and a measure of deference.

The world was polytheistic. Each province, each tribe and each family had their own gods. And your "god" was welcome as well. "You respect mine and I'll respect yours." Of course the teachings of Jesus would not allow this to His followers. When Christians proclaimed that their God was real and all others false, there was hell to pay. So trials and tribulations followed; Christians and pagans alike experienced the horrors of war and pillage. Both alike had to endure loss of life in children and loved ones. Both had suffered loss of children and other family members to the slave traders. Both suffered illness and death.

What did the pagans see in the response of the believers in Jesus?

Did they witness the grief and sorrow of loss of precious loved ones, of pain and suffering, as somehow triumphant, of victorious over the details of living, so that they were attractive? Was it the reality of the Christian experience in the vicissitudes of life, the power to endure and to prevail no matter what?

What we can know for sure is whatever it was, in the relatively short span of 2-300 years or so, Christianity had spread throughout the area of Europe, North Africa and the Middle East and is still continuing its spread today. The understood "Good News" is attractive. The foreigners saw the patience, courage, and faith exhibited by the Christians and that they lived not just for this life but also for another world. And Christians dying for their faith demonstrated that reality. Their faith was infectious.

How could those early Christians manage that and how can we? If the unbelieving world could see in us, the beauty of our Lord, they would fall in love with Him just as we have!

Which of us does not want to be able to rise above the troubles, disappointments, and heartbreak experienced on earth? We can remind ourselves of the early Christian's experience. The record shows they did not anticipate the resurrection, even though Jesus had taught on it repeatedly and at length. After the crucifixion, they were bewildered and uncertain. When the risen Lord appeared in the room with them, he entered miraculously, the doors being locked. The road to Emmaus account is illuminating (Luke 24).

Could we have been there, we would have seen them all in bug-eyed wonder. Picture this. The early Christian missionaries lived in the reality of that resurrection, even when they were second and third generations after. They were living in the reality of the brevity of our earthly life. What happened here, while important, was experienced from the perspective of eternity. Today, we strive for that mindset so that unbelievers can see the reality of our faith.

Not living in our own strength, of course, but we live in the reliability of Bible faith. This "witness" of triumphant living in spite of the ever present challenges of life, and dying with courage and faith and, in a sense, triumph, brought new believers into the fold. They too wanted to triumph over their harsh and unpromising circumstances.

What else could explain the rapid conversion of pagans to the faith? It was seeing the reality of the claims of the gospel being lived out in the kindness and generosity to others and the outworking of the new birth in Christ into the common experience of the downtrodden and poverty stricken, then as well as now.

The recognition that, as image-bearers of Christ and also seeing in others the same image bearing, provides the foundation for the immense dignity, significance, value, meaning and purpose that God has vested in each person. And the radical "dying to self" that is revealed and demonstrated in the life of Jesus. Patience in trials and suffering, and the fearless facing of death revealed the reality and the validity of following Christ.

The early Christians were living out the Sermon on the Mount (Matthew 5, 6, and 7). Many scholars view it as the greatest sermon ever preached. The audience was composed of very religious people. They were keepers of the law. They were doing the externals. Jesus was teaching on the need to move it from the merely external and plant it into our hearts.

Six times in chapter 5 Jesus said: "You have heard, or read, or it is written", and then said: "But I say:"

Verse 21 ...."Hate is as bad as murder."

Verse 27 ...."Lust is adultery in the heart."

Verse 31, 32 ....."Only one legitimate ground for divorce."

Verse 33 ...."Do not swear at all."

Verse 38, 39 ....."Not eye for eye but turn the other cheek."

Verse 44 ...."Love your enemies."

There is a passage in Matthew 5:41 about going the extra mile. The Roman soldier of that day could require a civilian to carry his pack one mile without compensation. The story is told of a soldier doing just that, and to his astonishment the lad offers to carry it a second mile. The soldier, walking alongside is reflecting on his years of soldiering and thinking "this has never happened to me before." And, wondering "why is this young lad doing this?" And he also wonders – "Why is he smiling?"

You and I know why! He is smiling because in serving the

soldier the extra mile – he is really serving his King, Jesus. Many acts and other things like this validated the Christian testimony! Lord grant that we too, would faithfully serve you in our lives so the watching world will see and know that we know You and be drawn to You.

As a young Christian I had it so wrong. I didn't drink or smoke or run around on my wife and I thought my job was to register my disapproval towards those who did! I now confess it as sin! It is Satan who is the accuser (Revelations 12:10). How sad! The devil convinces the world that we Christians think we are better than them, and don't like them...and probably even hate them! Lord have mercy on us. Lord, please grant that all our lives would reflect Your love to everyone! Historians have sought other explanations more in keeping with the secular views of the age, but none suffice or explain as well as the historic Biblical answer.

Review and Reflect

How can you use this to equip others to resist the God-denying and faith-destroying *theory* of evolution?

27

Religion Versus God

The variety and number of different religions in the world according to Wikipedia include, as of 2020AD are:

Christianity 31.1%

Islam 24.9%

Unaffiliated 15.6%

Hinduism 15.2%

Buddhism............. 6.6%

Folk religion 5.6%

Other 1.0%

If you generally describe religion as the search for God and the seeking to appease or find favor with God, properly speaking, Christianity does not fit in. Scripture reveals that, in Jesus Christ, God came seeking to save the lost while in other religions man is trying to measure up to some standard, to do some deed to find God's favor.

Compared to God's righteousness, again *"All men's*

righteousness are as filthy rags..." (Isaiah 64:6). It would not be surprising if it said all man's sins are rags. Our righteousness does not pay the sin debt. That is why it was necessary for the virgin birth, so that Jesus, born of the Holy Spirit would not have a sin nature, handed down the line from Adam through all our earthly fathers. "In Adam all die," (1 Corinthians 15:22).

So if you made a lengthy and comprehensive investigation to determine how Christianity differed from all other religions, what would you find? Many believe that religions are superficially different, but fundamentally the same. The reverse is true. Superficially they may appear similar but they are divided in what you must do to attain God's favor. The world's religions insist you must do something. They are *works*-based or *performance*-based. Scripture says to become a child of God you must *believe*. Believe what?

God says: That Christ died for you!

God says: That He doesn't have anything against you!

God says: That your sins were dealt with by the death of the Savior!

God says: You are lost and under His curse, but you don't have to remain that way!

God says: You do not have to deal with His justice and face Him in judgment!

God says: He loves you and He has broken down all the barriers between you and Him, and you can come to Him boldly on the grounds of His grace!

What is Grace?

Grace is unmerited favor, undeserved favor, and unearned

favor from God. In other religions we try to merit God's favor through our efforts, our dedication, and our denial of self. There is a place for human effort in Christianity, but not for earning of salvation! Salvation is a gift that the Lord Jesus graciously provided to those who would believe on His finished work on the cross and triumphant resurrection!

Lost mankind follows its own instincts seeking fulfillment in things, in achievements and attainments, but these satisfy only temporarily. Success, whether in business, sports, learning or finding your perfect mate, have the power to satisfy only for a while. We have a God-shaped vacuum in our lives that only God Himself can fill. Reconciliation with God, from our rebellions, sins and failures, is the ultimate fulfillment. "The water I give you shall be a springing up from your innermost being." (The woman at the well meets Jesus in John 4.)

The difference between Christianity and all others is GRACE. The price has been paid. The work has been done.

Our job is to believe. Are you willing?

Our response to grace is to believe. That is not all, but it is the first step. The enemy convinces the world that to believe in God is to suffer great diminishment in our opportunities for fulfillment and satisfaction. And in our childish response we agree. Just as the child having no conception of why another piece of chocolate is not necessarily a good thing, we look at the things that possess such allure and promise, and can hate or reject God for denying them to us.

Children have little in the way of restraint. If it feels good do it! Belief in Jesus Christ as God's provision for our reconciliation is our first step. After that we have the potential to grow into a more mature awareness of why God says "don't" to some things. God's laws are to keep us and others out of trouble. *Don't* means don't hurt yourself or other people. His rules are love-based and He loved us first while we were yet sinners! He deserves to be our First Love. He lovingly warns against putting anyone or thing in front of Him, not because He cannot handle the competition, but because He does not want His children settling for paltry counterfeits! And anything we put before Him becomes an idol!

Salvation is free and we can do nothing to earn it, or to contribute our part to salvation. It is the finished work of Jesus on the cross where He took upon Himself our sins and the punishment for our sins, and not ours only, but the sins of the whole world. So when the devil says you will experience great loss if you enter into this transaction of salvation, is there any sense at all in which that is right? Does belief in Jesus for salvation entail any kind of obligation, commitment, and any duty on our part? Is the devil partly right or only in the sense that we are to lose selfishness by loving God first and neighbors as ourselves?

The New Testament goes to great lengths to establish and to reiterate that God did it all and there is nothing anyone can add to it. Salvation is a gift which cannot be earned. It would not be a gift if we had to earn it. So, if I believe and receive do I somehow obligate myself in some way or in any way?

Others may differ, but I think not. Just as we have rebellious children in our earthly families, even so we can resist God's loving counsel about what is wise and what is not wise in our lives. That said, the new spiritual birth that God put within each believer inclines us to want to cooperate with God's will for our lives. The enemy cunningly equates religion with God, makes reference to all the atrocities committed by religion, and dismisses God in the process. Don't let them get away with it!

Review and Reflect

Can you digest the main points of God's salvation and share them with others?

28

Sometimes We Know More Than We Think!

A lecturer once asked his group how many could name the five great lakes. Of approximately two hundred, about a dozen raised their hands. "How many of you know the names of the great lakes," he asked. Again, about a dozen raised their hands. I'm persuaded that most of us know, but do not have a "memory device" to help us remember. "Try this," he said. "Picture H O M E S surrounding the lakes. Now tell me the names. Nearly two hundred voices answered:

Huron
Ontario
Michigan
Erie
Superior.

Next is a quiz of a different kind. You may do a lot better on it than you think. No peeking. Can you guess the person described in the following passages?

1. *"But thou, Bethlehem Ephrathah, though thou be little among the thousands of Judah, yet out of thee shall He come forth unto Me that shall be ruler in Israel; whose goings forth have been from old, from everlasting."* (Micah 5:2)

2. Therefore the Lord Himself shall give you a sign. *"Behold, a virgin shall conceive, and bear a son, and call His name Immanuel."* (Isaiah 7:14)

3. Isaiah, chapter 53. And to whom has the arm of the LORD been revealed?

   a. *For He shall grow up before Him as a tender plant, and as a root out of dry ground. He has no form or comeliness; and when we see Him, there is no beauty that we should desire Him.*

   b. *He is despised and rejected by men, a Man of sorrows and acquainted with grief. And we hid, as it were, our faces from Him; He was despised, and we did not esteem Him.*

   c. *Surely, He has borne our griefs and carried our sorrows; yet we esteemed Him stricken, smitten by God, and afflicted.*

   d. *But He was wounded for our transgressions, He was bruised for our iniquities; the chastisement for our peace was upon Him, and by His stripes we are healed.*

   e. *All we like sheep have gone astray; We have turned, every one, to his own way; And the LORD has laid on Him the iniquity of us all.*

   f. *He was oppressed and He was afflicted, yet He opened not His mouth; He was led as a lamb to the slaughter, and as a sheep before its shearers is silent, so He opened not His mouth.*

g. *He was taken from prison and from judgment, and who will declare His generation? For He was cut off from the land of the living; For the transgressions of My people, He was stricken.*

h. *And they made His grave with the wicked— but with the rich at His death, because He had done no violence, nor was any deceit in His mouth.*

i. *Yet it pleased the LORD to bruise Him; He has put Him to grief. When You make His soul an offering for sin, He shall see His seed, He shall prolong His days, and the pleasure of the LORD shall prosper in His hand.*

j. *He shall see the labor of His soul, and be satisfied. By His knowledge My righteous Servant shall justify many, for He shall bear their iniquities.*

k. *Therefore I will divide Him a portion with the great and He shall divide the spoil with the strong, because He poured out His soul unto death, and He was numbered with the transgressors, and He bore the sin of many, and made intercession for the transgressors.*

4. *Yea, mine own familiar friend in whom I trusted, which did eat of my bread, hath lifted up his heel against me.* (Psalms 41:95) *And I said unto them, if ye think good, give me my price, and if not, forbear. So they weighed for my price thirty pieces of silver.* (Zechariah 11:12)

5. *He was oppressed, and he was afflicted, yet he opened not his mouth....* (Isaiah 53:7)

6. *They pierced my hands and my feet.* (Psalms 22:16)

7. *And in my thirst they gave me vinegar to drink.* (Psalms 69:21)

8. *And they shall look on him whom they have pierced.* (Zechariah 12:10)

9. *They part my garment among them, and cast lots upon my vesture.* (Psalms 22:18)

10. *And he kept his bones; not one of them is broken.* (Psalms 34:20)

11. *Neither will thou suffer thine Holy One to see corruption.* (Psalms 16:10)

12. *Thou hast ascended on high, thou hast led captivity captive.* (Psalms 68:18)

Consider this from Daniel 9:

Know therefore and understand, that from the going forth of the command to restore and build Jerusalem until Messiah the Prince, there shall be seven weeks and sixty-two weeks; The street shall be built again, and the wall, even in troublesome times. And after the sixty-two weeks, Messiah shall be cut off but not for Himself; and the people of the prince who is to come Shall destroy the city and the sanctuary. (Fulfilled in 70 A.D.)

Yes, the passages do speak about Jesus Christ.

But there is something very striking and remarkable about them. See if you can tell from their source location?

All the passages are from THE (Old Testament) JEWISH TESTAMENT and are proven to have been written hundreds of years before the events happened as recorded in the Septuagint, a translation from the original Hebrew and Aramaic into Koine Greek. (circa 300-200BC)

When Alexander conquered the known world from Mediterranean Europe across Asia Minor to India, he refused to learn foreign languages and required the conquered people to speak and write in his language, Koine Greek.

Since it was translated two to three hundred years before the Birth of Christ, the passages are confirmed as authentic prophecy fulfilled as recorded in the New Testament.

One Solitary Life

A child is born in an obscure village. He is brought up in another obscure village. He works in a carpenter shop until He is thirty, and then for three brief years is an itinerant preacher, proclaiming a message and living a life. He never writes a book. He never holds an office. He never raises an army. He never has a family of His own. He never owns a home. He never goes to college. He never travels two hundred miles from the place where He was born. He gathers a little group of friends about Him and teaches them His way of life. While still a young man, the tide of popular feeling turns against Him. One denies Him; another betrays Him. He is turned over to His enemies. He goes through the mockery of a trial; He is nailed to a cross between two thieves, and when dead is laid in a borrowed grave by the kindness of a friend.

Those are the facts of His human life. He rises from the dead. Today we look back across nineteen hundred years and ask, what kind of trail has He left across the centuries? When we try to sum up His influence, all the armies that ever marched, all the parliaments that ever sat, all the kings that ever reigned are absolutely picayune in their influence on mankind compared with that of this One solitary life...

— Dr. James Allan Francis

"I am trying here to prevent anyone saying the really foolish thing that people often say about Him: I'm ready to accept Jesus as a great moral teacher, but I don't accept His claim to be God. That is the one thing we must not say. A man who was merely a man and said the sort of things Jesus said would not be a great moral teacher. He would either be a lunatic — on the level with the man who says he is a poached egg — or else He would be the Devil of Hell. You must make your choice. Either this man was, and is, the Son of God, or else a madman or something worse. You can shut Him up for a fool, you can spit at Him and kill Him as a demon or you can fall at his feet and call him Lord and God, but let us not come with any patronizing nonsense about His being a great human teacher. He has not left that open to us. He did not intend to."

— C.S. Lewis, Mere Christianity

The time is now. The Goliath of our time, the *theory* of evolution appears as a colossal and invincible fortress astride and ruling the world. Are the preceding thoughts enough to help destroy confidence in the *theory* in the minds of the church, and of our children? David declared "The battle is the Lord's" and killed the giant.

> *The weapons of our warfare are not carnal, but mighty through God, to the pulling down of strong holds.* (2 Corinthians 10:4)

You are David! Here are your stones! Go slay Goliath!

Simon Greenleaf

In the year 1833, Simon Greenleaf "rocked the boat" of law and evidence, that even had a great effect on our modern-day apologetics.

He was named to the Royal professorship, and in 1846 succeeded Judge Joseph Story as Dane professor of law at Harvard University. Professor Greenleaf contributed extensively to the development of Harvard Law School, including expansion of the Harvard Law Library. He was retained as chief counsel by the Warren Bridge Group in the United States Supreme Court case Charles River Bridge v. Warren Bridge 36 U.S. 420 (1837), where the case decided the rule that public contracts must be construed in favor of states.

In 1848, Greenleaf retired from his active duties at Harvard, and was named professor emeritus. After being for many years president of the Massachusetts Bible Society, he died at Cambridge. Greenleaf's well-known work, a *Treatise on the Law of Evidence*, is considered a cornerstone and classic of American jurisprudence.

The three volumes I have: *A Treaty on the Law of Evidence* is the fifteenth edition copyrighted in 1892 A.D. Volume One is 784 pages, Volume Two is 674 pages, and Volume Three 584 Pages.

Greenleaf is an prominent figure in the development of the Christian school of thought known as *legal or juridical apologetics*. This school of thought is evidenced by legally-trained scholars applying the canons of proof and argument to the defense of our Christian faith. Greenleaf's *Testimony of the Evangelists* became the model for many subsequent works by legal apologists.

Most notably, he is distinguished as one who applied the canons of the ancient document rule to establish the authenticity of the New Testament Gospel accounts, as well as cross-examination principles in assessing the testimony of those who bore witness to the crucifixion and resurrection of Jesus. In fact, his style of reasoning is reflected in the apologetic works by Josh McDowell, John Warwick Montgomery, and Ross Clifford.

Greenleaf's Other Writings

Greenleaf's principal work of legal scholarship is a *Treatise on the Law of Evidence* (3 volumes, 1842–1853), which remained a standard textbook in American law throughout the nineteenth century. He also published *A Full Collection of Cases Overruled, Denied, Doubted, or Limited in their Application*, taken from American and English Reports in 1821. Additionally, he prepared and published *Reports of Cases Argued and Determined by the Supreme Judicial Court of the State of Maine* in nine volumes (1820–1832). He revised, for the American courts, William Cruise's *Digest of Laws Respecting Real Property* (3 volumes, 1849–1850).

Greenleaf was also the author of *A Brief Inquiry*, and wrote a memoir of the life of his colleague Joseph Story - *A Discourse Commemorative of the Life and Character of the Hon. Joseph Story* (1845 mentioned by actress <u>Marium Carvell</u>, playing Selma Davis, in *Judgment*, a.k.a. *Apocalypse IV*).

Simon Greenleaf literally wrote the book the courts used as the standard for what was and was not allowed in the courts of the United States during the latter part of the nineteenth century.

His later book, *The Testimony of the Evangelists* found the New Testament records so reliable that they fulfilled and satisfied all the standards of his landmark work, which was the standard for what was admissible in the court. It was copyrighted in 1995 by Kregel Classics, Grand Rapids, Michigan. Read it and see for yourself.

The enemies of God may continue to bring all kinds of spurious charges against the New Testament. You can rely on expert testimony that the record is trustworthy.

Now what? Scripture records that two men walked on water. Jesus and who else? You know, don't you? Simon Peter. Some have poked fun at Peter because he had to have help getting back into the boat. But he did have faith to get out of the boat. Would you? Don't be too sure. Most of us are not even willing to "rock the boat." Develop boldness and confidence with what you now know.

Go out there and ROCK THE BOAT!